THE ✸ TIMES

BEGINNER'S GUIDE TO BRIDGE

Published by Collins
An imprint of HarperCollins Publishers
Westerhill Road
Bishopbriggs
Glasgow G64 2QT

First Edition 2015

Previously published as *Collins Need to Know? Bridge*. Now with additional practice deals.

ISBN 978-0-00-813094-7

10 9 8 7 6 5 4 3 2 1

www.harpercollins.co.uk

The Times is a registered trademark of Times Newspapers Ltd

Typeset by Davidson Publishing Solutions

Printed in Great Britain by Clays Ltd, St Ives plc

Inside card illustrations © Pascal Thivillon

A catalogue record for this book is available from the British Library.

If you would like to comment on any aspect of this book, please contact us at the given address or e-mail puzzles@harpercollins.co.uk.

To my mother and father, who got me started.

Andrew Robson, 2015

Contents

Welcome to bridge

Bridge is possibly the best game devised by mankind – and certainly one of the most popular. But a word of warning: you'll soon be hooked. Fortunately, this need not be expensive and will be good both for your brain and your social life.

First steps

This book will please complete beginners, as no assumption of prior knowledge has been made. It's also suitable for those who play social 'kitchen' bridge and want to develop their game.

The first chapter ('Appetiser') starts from scratch. By the end of it you'll understand the essence of the game and be able to play, though at a rudimentary level. Those who have played before may prefer to skim these pages. The second chapter ('Basics') gives guidelines for bidding and card play. Work through this and you'll have done the equivalent of completing the eight-week beginner course at my bridge club. In the third chapter ('Core'), each area of the game is considered in more detail, taking you to intermediate-level bridge. Chapter 4 ('Development') takes things further, revealing the ingenuity – and sheer beauty – of the game. Finally, you'll find information on scoring in chapter 5, and details of different types of bridge and bidding styles.

My suggestion is to read chapters 1 and 2, then try to get some practice – even if it's just dealing out cards by yourself (a very stimulating and productive thing to do). At this stage, although probably not the strongest player at the table, you'll be able to play a perfectly adequate game of social bridge; best of all, you'll be having fun. When you're ready, move on to chapters 3 and 4, using chapter 5 as a reference when you want to know more about scoring.

A short history

A trick-taking game, bridge evolved from whist, which has been played for centuries. The first book devoted to whist, *Edmond Hoyle's Short Treatise*, appeared in 1742 and became a bestseller.

No one knows the roots of the name 'bridge'. It may have evolved from 'biritch', the name of a Russian game with similar rules, or possibly the Turkish term 'bir uc', meaning 'one-three' – as in one exposed hand and three concealed ones.

In 1903 British civil servants in India developed the practice of bidding for the privilege of naming the trump suit, thus introducing 'Auction bridge'. 'Contract bridge', the universally played modern form, was only formally invented in 1925: not in a seedy back room, but on an American cruise ship under the guidance of Harold Vanderbilt. US marketer Ely Culbertson soon popularized the game, and by 1930 it was *the* society activity on both sides of the Atlantic. Since those first heady days, bridge has made front page news – when a famous British pair, Reese and Schapiro, were accused of cheating in 1965. It has attracted film stars – Omar Sharif played at the top level – and featured in many books, perhaps the most famous of all being Ian Fleming's *Moonraker*. Bill Gates and Warren Buffett are keen bridge players, and if they give just a small fraction of their wealth back to the game, we can look forward to a very bright future, especially as bridge is now more widely accessible than ever – via the internet.

Useful tip

Bridge is a ceaselessly fascinating and stimulating game. Start playing by partnering someone more experienced than you, who can help you get the most out of your play.

1 Appetiser

If you feel daunted by the complicated techniques and rules of bridge, just remember that it's a game which can be enjoyed at any level. This chapter sets out the preliminary steps you need to make to have your first game of bridge.

The mechanics

Bridge is a partnership game. The 'bidding', the first phase of the game, establishes a target number of tricks to be made by each partnership. During the second phase, the partnership that wins the bidding tries to achieve their target number of tricks; the defending partnership tries to stop them.

must know

Spades and hearts are the higher-ranking and higher-scoring suits, known as the 'majors'; diamonds and clubs are the lower-ranking and lower-scoring suits, known as the 'minors'.

Cards and ranking

Bridge is played with a standard pack of cards. The ace is the highest (or best) card of each suit – the two is the lowest. The ranking of suits is in reverse alphabetical order, as shown below: clubs are ranked the lowest, then diamonds, hearts and spades – the highest. Most social bridge, or 'Rubber Bridge' (the different types of bridge are explained on pp. 228–31), is played with two packs of cards that are distinguishable by the colour (design) on the backs.

Ranking order

Highest card · Lowest card

Drawing for partners and dealer

Bridge is a game for four people (two partnerships) seated round a table. Their positions are often referred to as points of the compass: North, South, East and West. To decide on partners (if you don't wish to choose), and who deals first, each player draws a card, placing it face up on the table. Whoever draws the highest card deals first, chooses where to sit and ushers the player who draws the second highest card to be their partner. Partners sit opposite.

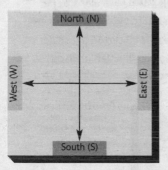

The position of partners at the table

Shuffling and dealing etiquette

The dealer chooses which of the two packs he wishes to deal. Before dealing commences, the opponent to the left of the dealer (LHO – West in the example opposite) shuffles the chosen pack and places it on the dealer's left; meanwhile the partner of the dealer (sitting opposite) shuffles the other pack and places it on their right. The dealer then picks up the shuffled pack on their left, shuffles it again (this is optional) and passes it to the opponent on their right (RHO – East in the example opposite) to be 'cut'. RHO cuts the pack by lifting (very approximately) half the cards, placing the top half on the table nearer the dealer and leaving the bottom half where it is. The cards are

After the shuffle, showing South as the dealer; the pack is cut by East

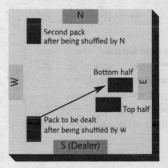

now ready to be dealt. The dealer takes the part of the pack furthest away from him and puts it on top of the closer part (known as 'completing the cut'). He then picks up the pack (face down) and gives the top card (face down) to LHO, the next card to his partner opposite, the next to RHO, then one to himself, and so on in clockwise rotation, until all 52 cards have been dealt. The last card is always to the dealer.

When the next deal occurs (after all 52 cards have been played and 13 tricks won - see below), this is done with the other pack. The new dealer is to the left of the previous dealer (in clockwise rotation). As before, the pack to be dealt is placed on the dealer's left, shuffled by the person on their left, then cut towards the dealer by the person on their right.

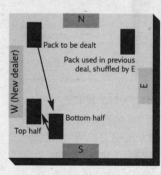

The next deal: West is the new dealer and South cuts the cards

A trick

Bridge involves taking tricks. A trick consists of one card from each player. Each player holds 13 cards, making 13 tricks per deal. The more tricks you and your partner win, the better; your side needs to win a minimum of seven tricks in the deal in order to score points towards a game (see pp. 220–4 for more on the points required to make a game).

One player has the lead for each trick, i.e. he or she plays the first card of the trick. For the first trick, the player on lead is seated to the left of the dealer; for the next and later tricks it is the player who won the previous trick.

After the opening lead, the play proceeds in clockwise order. If you hold a card in the same suit as the first card of the trick then you must play it ('follow suit'). If not, you can play any card of another suit: unless it's a trump card (see p. 12), a card of a another suit will not win you the trick so you will generally 'throw away' a low card.

The highest card in the lead suit wins the trick. If a trump card is played to a trick led in another suit, the highest card of the trump suit – rather than the highest card in the lead suit – wins the trick. Whoever wins the trick leads to the next trick.

In (a) opposite, East can choose any card to lead; he chooses ♥3. The other players must follow suit, i.e. play a card in the lead suit (hearts) – if they have a card in that suit. Play proceeds clockwise, with South playing second, West third and North last. West wins the trick and leads to the next trick.

In the next trick (b), North plays the winning card, ♣Q. East, North's opponent, plays a low card (♣4) because he doesn't have a ♣K or ♣A to beat North's ♣Q. South, on the other hand, would not waste a high card to overtake ♣Q because she is in partnership with North, who is already winning the trick.

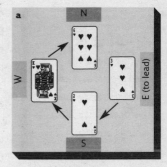

A trick won by West

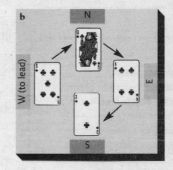

The next trick is won by North

must know
Everything in bridge is done clockwise, for example, dealing and play proceed in clockwise order – and bidding too.

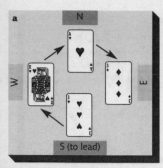

Trumps are diamonds

Overtrumping with clubs as trumps

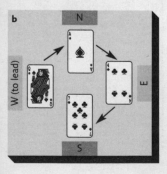

A trump

Cards in the trump (or 'boss') suit outrank all other cards. The trump suit is determined during the first phase of the game – the bidding.

Look again at (a) on p. 11. Imagine that North is about to play the last card to the trick. There are two ways he can win this trick. First, if he holds ♥A then this will beat his opponent's ♥K. Second, if he doesn't hold ♥A, and he has no other hearts in his hand, then he can (but is not compelled to) play a card of the trump suit, if one has been chosen. With a trump card he will automatically win the trick, even if he trumps with the lowly two.

In (a) on this page, diamonds are trumps and South (who won the previous trick) leads. When West's ♥K is beaten by North's ♥A, West's partner, East, comes to the rescue: East has no hearts so can trump with ♦3, which wins the trick.

Overtrumping

If another player trumps, and you (also) have no cards in the lead suit, you have the option of overtrumping that player. In (b), clubs are trumps and West leads. South doesn't hold a spade so can overtrump East's ♣4 with ♣7, and win the trick. Note that if East had followed with a spade, South would not need to trump because his partner (North) would be winning the trick with ♠A.

Your 13 cards – your 'hand'

Once the cards have been dealt you can pick up your cards and sort them into suits. Place the highest card at one end of each suit, the lowest card at the other. Split up the colours (black-red-black-red or red-black-red-black) to avoid muddling the suits; hearts and diamonds are particularly easy to confuse.

The diagram opposite shows a typical bridge hand, in ranking order. To save space, this will generally be represented as:

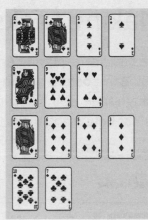

♠KJ32 ♥Q94 ♦J653 ♣107

Notice the distribution, or 'shape', of the hand. It contains a four-card suit, a three-card suit, a two-card suit and another four-card suit. The number of cards in each suit determines the suit 'length' – a shorter length has fewer cards; a longer length has more cards. Rearranging the suit lengths, in the example we have a 4432 distribution. The more you play, the more you'll realize that distribution is the key to bridge and can more than compensate for a low point score (see below).

Counting points

There is a unique method in bridge of evaluating the power of your hand – its trick-taking potential – based on the high cards. For each ace, the best card in the suit, you count four points, each king counts three, each queen is two and each jack (knave) one. No points are counted for tens and below.

As soon as you've sorted your hand and noted its distribution, you should count your points. There are 40 points in the whole pack – four aces, four kings, four queens and four jacks. The average number of points in any one hand is ten (one ace, one king, one queen and one jack). The hand in the diagram above contains only seven points; if this were yours you should hope that your partner has a few more points.

Useful tip
Tens and nines may not count as points, but they are nevertheless potentially useful cards, and better than twos and threes.

Making tricks

The basic card-playing principles involved in making tricks are best learnt before tackling the bidding part of bridge – even though the bidding occurs first in practice. They will give you a feel for how many tricks to aim for at the bidding stage.

Counting tricks

The partnership that wins the bidding contracts to make a certain number of tricks during the play phase of bridge. Within this partnership there is a 'declarer' and a 'dummy' (for more on these roles, see pp. 22–3). The declarer controls his own hand and dummy's (his partner's) hand, playing cards from both to try and achieve their trick target. In the following examples, imagine you are playing the role of the declarer and see how many tricks you can expect to make by playing out the suit in each case:

In (a), you can make three tricks if you play just one high card per trick. In (b), you can make four tricks by playing one high card for each of the four rounds. In (c), although you have the six top clubs, you must follow suit and can make only three tricks overall.

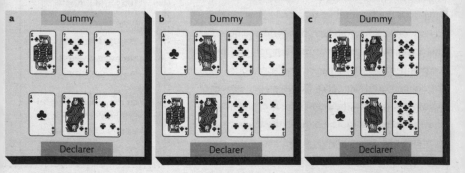

Which order to take ('cash') the tricks

In the examples on p. 14, it doesn't matter which hand is the declarer or the dummy, or from which you lead first. However, in many real-life cases, the order in which you play the cards is important if you want to make the maximum number of tricks available.

In (a) above, where there's an unequal number of cards in the two hands, there are three available tricks to be made, one after the other, but only if you cash them in the correct order. If you play ♦A first (or ♦4 to ♦A), you will then have to lead ♦2 to ♦K – because the hand winning the previous trick always leads to the next trick – and will be stuck in the wrong hand, unable to win ♦Q. To avoid being 'blocked' in this way, lead ♦K (or ♦2 to ♦K) first, then follow with ♦4 to ♦AQ.

In (b), you should play ♦Q and ♦5 on the first round, then ♦3 to ♦AKJ. Only in this way can you make four consecutive diamond tricks.

In (c), lead ♦2 to ♦K (or ♦K to ♦2). Follow with ♦J and ♦5, then ♦6 over to ♦AQ.

Note that these examples assume your opponents do not have a trump card that would win the trick (more on the use of trump cards on pp. 18–19).

(more on the use of trump cards on pp. 18–19).

must know

The Unblocking Rule (a guideline for cashing winners in the right order):
• If leading from the hand with the shorter length, lead the highest card.
• If leading from the hand with the longer length, lead the lowest card.

You may find it helpful to remember 'L' for 'Lead Longest Lowest'.

Extra tricks by force

So far you have cashed your 'top' tricks and your opponents have not had a look-in. Now consider the next three examples. In each case you are missing a high, winning card (or cards), and in order to make tricks in the suit you must 'force' out that card from the opposition partnership.

In (a), you are missing ♠A and need to force it out from the opposition. You can use any high card in the suit to do this, then go on to win the other two high cards when you regain the lead. In this way you promote two tricks by 'force'. Note that if your opponent withholds their ♠A on the first round, you'll win the trick anyway, effectively 'promoting' the high card you use to lead. You can then sacrifice a second high card in order to promote the third. Both scenarios give you your two tricks.

Example (b) contains the same high cards but in this case it's better to start specifically with ♠Q (or ♠7 to ♠Q) to force out ♠A. You'll then hold ♠2 in one hand and ♠KJ in the other, which avoids 'blockage'.

In (c), you need to force out ♠A and ♠K. To do this, sacrifice two of your sequential cards ♠Q, ♠J, ♠10, ♠9 (note that sequential cards between your hand and dummy's are worth the same). Then you have promoted the two cards that remain into two force winners.

Extra tricks by length

If you can exhaust your opponents of all of their cards in a suit, then your remaining cards, however small, will be promoted into 'length' winners. Assuming your opponents have no outstanding trumps, these remaining cards will be extra tricks.

In (a) below, you have four 'top' tricks (tricks made consecutively, with high ranking cards), but it would be very unlucky if you didn't also score ♥2. Your opponents hold five hearts between them. Unless they are all in one hand, they'll all fall when you win ♥AKQJ. ♥2 will then be a fifth-round winner – by virtue of its length. This scenario depends on how the five missing hearts are split between the opposition. If they're split 3-2 (most likely), or 4-1, you'll achieve your extra trick by length. The only problem will be the much less likely 5-0 split.

In (b) start with ♥Q (or ♥2 to ♥Q), as it's the highest card from the shorter length. Then lead ♥3 back to ♥J, and cash ♥A and ♥K. The six missing

Useful tip
Don't be overly concerned about losing the lead, particularly early in the play. You have to lose to win in bridge.

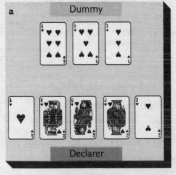

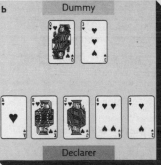

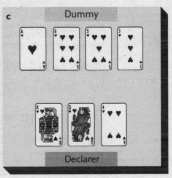

must know
Length before strength – a general rule to follow in bridge: having more cards in a suit is often more important than a higher point count.

cards in the suit will go in these four rounds if the
cards are split 3-3 or 4-2. Assuming they are (you'll
develop a habit of counting missing cards as they're
played), you can enjoy a length winner with ♥4.
A 5-1 split, however, would prevent this. Fortunately,
this is much less likely.

In (c), you have three top tricks but may also make
a fourth-round length winner. There are six missing
cards, held by the opposition. If the split is 3-3 (three
cards in each opposition hand), you have the chance
to enjoy a low-card length winner. Start with ♥K
(or ♥3 to ♥K), then ♥Q, then ♥4 to ♥A. If all six
missing hearts fall (i.e. both opponents follow suit
all three times), then ♥6 will be a length winner.
You'll be less lucky if the suit splits 4-2 (or 5-1 or
6-0) as there'll be an outstanding heart, which is
bound to be higher than your ♥6.

Trumping

Apart from length winners, the only way to make
tricks with twos and threes is by trumping. Which
suit is preferable here as trumps: ♠AKQ or ♣65432?
The answer is clubs because ♠AKQ rate to score tricks
whether or not they are trumps, whereas the only way
the small clubs are likely to win is by being trumps.
A key challenge of bidding is to discover which one of
the four suits holds the greatest combined length
between your partnership, as it will probably be best
to make that suit trumps.

Drawing trumps

When 'declaring' (playing the role of the declarer),
it's often good to get rid of the opposition's trumps
near the beginning of the hand so they can't trump

your winners. This is called 'drawing trumps'. You should avoid continuing playing your trumps (wasting two together) once your opponents have run out of theirs. You therefore need to count.

Counting trumps

First work out how many trumps are missing, then think of that missing number in terms of how the cards may be split between the opposition partners, bearing in mind that they'll usually have approximately the same number as each other. Each time you see an opponent play a trump, mentally reduce the number of missing trumps by one.

In the example below, the declarer counts five missing trumps. He cashes ♠K and, when he sees both opponents follow suit, reduces his mental count of missing trumps down to three. ♠2 to ♠Q draws two more of the opponents' trumps. There's just one more left out (and it's now obvious that the split is 3–2). The declarer cashes ♠A, drawing the last trump, and doesn't need to play a fourth round in the trump suit.

must know
Counting trumps is important. Once you have drawn trumps from your opponents, i.e. exhausted them of their trump cards, you should stop playing in the trump suit and turn to others. Carrying on playing in the trump suit would be a waste because your remaining trumps could probably be made separately, by trumping another suit.

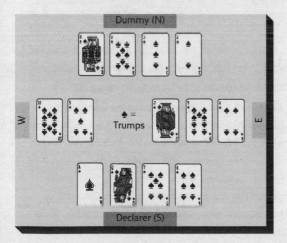

Introducing the bidding

Each bid carries a message and is used to tell your partner what type of hand you have: its strength and which suit(s), if any, you'd like as trumps. Your aim is to outbid the other side with a final bid, a 'contract' or trick target, that suits both you and your partner's hands (hence the term 'contract' bridge – see p. 228).

(hence the term 'contract' bridge – see p. 228)

must know

By the end of the bidding, the following will be determined:
- whether the deal will be played in a trump suit (clubs, diamonds, hearts or spades), or without a trump suit ('no-trumps' – see p. 27);
- how many tricks need to be made by the side who has bid highest and therefore won the contract; and, by deduction, how many tricks their opponents need in order to stop them from winning;
- which player within the highest bidding partnership is the declarer, and which is the dummy.

Opening the bidding

The bidding starts with the dealer, who decides whether to 'open the bidding'. If he has an average or worse-than-average hand, he says 'no bid' or 'pass'. If he has a better-than-average hand (12 points is a good guide), he opens the bidding by stating his preferred suit as trumps – choosing one of his longest suits.

In (a), the dealer says 'Pass' as he has only ten points (an average point score as there are 40 points in the pack divided between four players).

a

Dealer's hand: ♠AQ62 ♥K4 ♦J963 ♣1076

Dealer says: 'Pass'

In (b), the dealer has 14 points – enough to open the bidding. He has more spades than any other suit, and would like spades to be trumps, so he opens 'One spade' (see p. 21, 'Making a bid at the One level').

b

Dealer's hand: ♠Q10753 ♥K3 ♦AK43 ♣Q2

Dealer says: 'One spade'

Once the dealer has bid (or passed), the bidding moves to the next player in clockwise rotation. If the dealer has passed, the second bidder now follows the same process as the dealer: with less than 12 points, he passes, with 12 or more he opens 'One...' followed by the name of his longest suit. The third and fourth bidders similarly need 12 points to open the bidding. Occasionally, when the high cards are evenly distributed, none of the four players will hold 12 or more points. The deal is then 'thrown in', and the next player in clockwise rotation deals with the other pack.

After the bidding has opened

Once the bidding has opened, 12 points are no longer needed to bid. You can enter the bidding if you have a good, long suit. There are two options: to make a higher bid – going up the series of steps shown in the diagram on p. 22 – or to pass. Note that your bid *must* be higher than the previous one. This is where the ranking order of suits is crucial: you can bid a higher-ranked suit or 'no-trumps' (a deal played without a trump suit – see p. 27) at the same level (e.g. at the One level), but to bid a lower-ranked suit you must 'raise the level' i.e. 'contract for' (promise to win) one more trick than the previous bidder.

The bidding continues until three players in a row pass, which signifies the end of the auction.

must know
Bidding essentials:
• Open the bidding with 12+ points.
• Once the bidding has opened, 12+ points are no longer needed to make a bid.
• You have two choices: to make a higher bid, or to pass (as in any other auction).
• The player within the highest-bidding partnership who was first to name the trump suit (or no-trumps) becomes the declarer. His partner becomes dummy.
• The defender on the left of the declarer leads the first card.

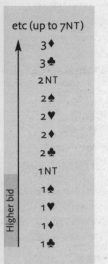

etc (up to 7NT)

3♦

3♣

2NT

2♠

2♥

2♦

2♣

1NT

1♠

1♥

1♦

1♣

Higher bid

The bidding steps: the number next to the suit refers to the number of tricks plus six that you are contracting to make in the chosen trump suit, or in no-trumps (NT)

must know

Bridge is a co-operative game: try to inform your partner about your hand, remembering that quantity is more important than quality when it comes to suggesting a trump suit. Bridge is also a competitive game: your opponents are trying to make your life awkward. Do not be fooled or bullied by them.

After the bidding has ended

Each of the four players has the opportunity to bid on the first round. When the bidding ends (three passes in a row), the highest bid becomes the final contract, and the player who first bid the suit (within the highest-bidding partnership) becomes the declarer. The player on the declarer's left leads the first card (choosing any card to lead). The declarer's partner then puts down his hand face up, sorted into suits (his hand is 'tabled'), and, as the 'dummy', takes no further part in playing out the deal, the declarer playing cards

A typical bidding sequence

North deals and passes as he lacks 12+ points needed to open the bidding. East (next in clockwise rotation) opens the bidding with 1♥ – he has 12+ points and his longest (or equal longest) suit is hearts. South then bids 2♣ – he doesn't need 12 points as the bidding has opened, but must raise the level to 'Two' (i.e. an eight-trick target) because clubs are ranked lower than hearts. West supports his partner's chosen suit, hearts, by bidding 2♥, North then bids 3♣, upping his partnership's target to nine winning tricks out of thirteen. North's 3♣ bid ends the auction, because it is followed by three passes in a row, and 3♣ becomes the final contract. South becomes declarer and must make nine (or more) tricks with clubs as trumps; the defenders E-W need to win five tricks in order to stop him.

from his own hand and from the dummy hand. Thus, everyone playing the deal is able to see half the deck: 13 cards in their own hand and the 13 cards laid out on the table by dummy. The advantage for the declarer is that he is the only player at the table who can see his own partner's cards, and gets to play them.

In the example below, South becomes declarer (by virtue of bidding the trump suit, clubs, first). West, on his left, leads, whereupon dummy (North) tables his cards face up, placing trumps (clubs) on his right, and the other suits (preferably with colours split) to his left, with the highest card in each suit nearest dummy, the lowest nearest the middle of the table.

After the play

Either the declarer fulfils his target (perhaps even making extra tricks), or he doesn't (because he fails to achieve the contracted number of tricks, by one or more). All eventualities are taken into consideration in the scoring (see pp. 220-7).

want to know more?
• The type of bridge described in this book is 'Rubber Bridge', a version of Contract Bridge whose overall objective is to win a 'rubber', i.e. the best of three games. For more on scoring games and rubbers, see pp. 220-7.
• Other types of bridge, including Chicago, Duplicate and Minibridge, are outlined on pp. 228-31.
• Other methods of evaluating a bridge hand (besides counting points) are covered on pp. 190-5.

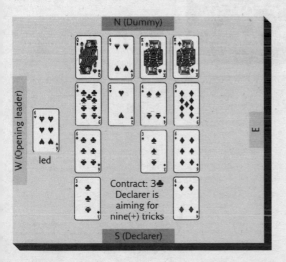

Dummy is tabled

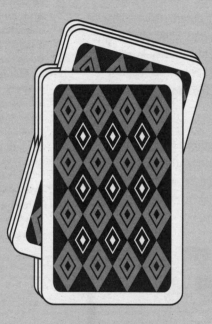

2 Basics

By now you've had your first taste of bridge and you're ready to move on. You're learning that distribution, or 'shape', is the key to bridge. In this chapter you'll learn more about assessing a bridge hand, finding a trump fit and bidding to a game contract. There's also guidance on trick-taking and defence.

Bidding

In bidding, your objective is to indicate to your partner what sort of hand you have, and determine how many tricks to aim for. To open the bidding we've learnt that you need 12 or more points. If you are able to open, you must also see if your hand is balanced or unbalanced: your whole bidding strategy depends on the answer.

Balanced or unbalanced hand?

The 13 cards of each suit are divided between between the four players. Each hand has a distribution, for example, a hand consisting of three spades, three hearts, four diamonds and three clubs has a distribution of 4333.

> A balanced hand contains:
> - no void (suit with no cards)
> - no 'singleton' (suit with just one card)
> - not more than one 'doubleton' (suit with just two cards)

The distributions, or shapes, that satisfy all three criteria are 4432, 4333 and 5332. These are the three balanced shapes (below):

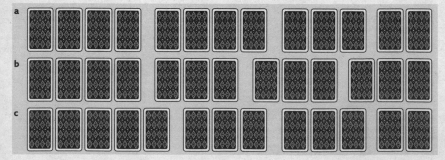

Opening with a balanced hand

With a balanced hand – no void, no singleton and not
more than one doubleton – your bidding plan should
revolve around no-trumps (see below). The even spread
of a balanced hand means you have no strong preference
for a trump suit, which is why bidding no-trumps makes
sense. However, an opening bid of One no-trump (1NT)
shows a specific point count, so you may need to delay
your no-trump bid if your point count is higher in order
to convey the right message to your partner.

No-trumps

As the name suggests, 'no-trumps' means that the deal is played without a trump suit so in
each round played the highest card of the lead suit always wins the trick. Arguably it's
slightly more difficult for the declaring side not to have the security of a trump suit, but no
trumps outranks all the trump suits (see the bidding ladder on p. 22 and notice that no-
trumps is higher ranked than spades, the highest ranked suit). No-trumps also scores
slightly better (see p. 221), so plays a huge role. Typically, a no-trump bid is made when you
have no long suit and no short suit – an even spread, or balanced hand. The most important
no-trump bid is the opening bid of One no-trump (1NT) because this describes your hand
very accurately to your partner. If you open the bidding with 1NT, in most cases you
shouldn't bid again. Having described your hand so accurately, you should leave further
bidding decisions to your partner (see p. 35 for your partner's response to a 1NT opener).

If you have a balanced hand with 12, 13 or 14 points,
you should open the bidding with One no-trump
(1NT). In (a) on the next page, all three hands are 1NT
openers. In (b), none of the three hands should
open 1NT. The first has too many points (15) so
opening 1NT would paint too pessimistic a picture
for your partner. Instead you should open One-of-
a-suit (1♦ in this case) and plan to bid no-trumps at
your next turn. The second hand has just eleven

points, so you should pass. The third contains two doubletons: an unbalanced hand. In this case you should open 1♦.

(a) Examples of One no-trump (1NT) opening hands

(b) Examples of opening hands that are not One no-trump (1NT)

Now let's consider your opening strategy with these three balanced opening hands:

(a)	(b)	(c)
♠ AJ852	♠ A32	♠ AK74
♥ KQ9	♥ KJ85	♥ AQ3
♦ K105	♦ AKJ	♦ KJ62
♣ 85	♣ 863	♣ A9

(a) You have 13 points so should open 1NT. Leave further bidding to your partner (except in certain situations that we'll discuss later).

(b) You have 16 points – too many to open 1NT. You should open 1♥, then show your balanced hand by bidding 1NT at your next turn. By bidding a suit followed by no-trumps you're indicating to your partner that you have a balanced hand but with too many points to open 1NT (though not enough to open 2NT).

(c) You have 21 points. When your hand has 20+ points (i.e. at least half the pack's total points in your hand alone) you should tell the good news to your partner by opening at the level of 'Two' (2NT).

Useful tip
If you have 20+ points, open at the Two level (to remember, think 'Two-Twenty').

Strategy for opening bidding (balanced hand)
With a balanced hand (a distribution of 5332, 4432 or 4333), your opening bidding strategy should be:

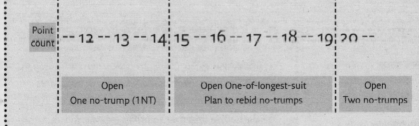

Point count	12 – 13 – 14	15 – 16 – 17 – 18 – 19	20 –
	Open One no-trump (1NT)	Open One-of-longest-suit Plan to rebid no-trumps	Open Two no-trumps

Opening with an unbalanced hand
If your opening hand is unbalanced (i.e. the distribution is not 4432, 4333 or 5332), then you should avoid bidding no-trumps at your first two bids.

Strategy for opening bidding (unbalanced hand)

With an unbalanced hand (not a distribution of 5332, 4432 or 4333), your opening bidding strategy should be:

Point count	-- 12 -- 13 -- 14 -- 15 -- 16 -- 17 -- 18 -- 19	20 --
	Open One-of-longest-suit	Open Two-of longest-suit

We'll consider these strategies in more detail later. For now, just remember that your aim is to describe your hand as accurately as possible to your partner, and if your partner responds in a new suit, you are obliged to bid again.

Finding a fit (making a suit trumps)

There are two primary goals of the bidding:

- To find a trump suit mutually agreeable to you and your partner – this is known as 'finding a fit'.
- To decide how many tricks to aim for in that chosen trump suit (or no-trumps) – in particular, whether to bid to a game contract.

When finding a fit, there is a minimum number of cards that should be held between you and your partner to warrant making a suit trumps. Clearly, it would be nice to hold all 13 cards in a suit, but this is rare. Eight cards is more likely and considered the

must know

- Introducing a suit into the bidding guarantees at least four cards in the suit are held by the bidder.
- A 'fit' means that a minimum of eight cards in one suit are held by the partnership.

minimum to make a good trump suit. This leaves the opponents with five cards in the suit (probably splitting 3-2 between the opposition partners), giving you a substantial advantage.

Three ways the suit cards may be distributed between the partnership for there to be a 'fit'

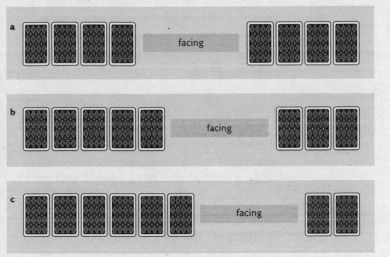

A common scenario is that your partner bids a suit, because he holds at least four cards in the suit. You also hold four (plus) cards in the suit so you know there's a fit. You then decide how many tricks to aim for – particularly whether or not to 'go for game'.

Bidding to a game contract

Bidding to a game contract, known as 'bidding game' or 'going for game', is very important. In Rubber Bridge, one game made marks a halfway point to the ultimate goal: scoring a rubber (see pp. 220–4).

The five game contracts are 3NT, 4♥, 4♠, 5♣ and 5♦. The game contract requiring the fewest tricks to win is 3NT (six plus three = nine tricks out of a total of thirteen – see the bidding steps on p. 22), which is

must know
You can make (win) a game either by making several small contracts ('part-scores') that add up to the score for game over several deals, or by making game in just one deal (a 'game contract'). For more on part-scores and game contracts, see p. 60.

why it's the most commonly played game contract – closely followed by 4♥ and 4♠. The last two (5♣ and 5♦) are more difficult and should be avoided.

A rough guide for bidding game is if your opening bid faces a hand that could also have opened the bidding (i.e. your partner also has 12 or more points), then your partnership should go for game. For example, South is dealer and he and his partner hold the following cards:

North	South
♠ AQJ2	♠ K3
♥ K4	♥ A52
♦ Q1052	♦ KJ43
♣ J75	♣ Q832

South has a balanced hand with 13 points – he opens the bidding 1NT. With the opponents silent, North, who also has an opening hand, immediately thinks 'game'. With no particular preference for a trump suit (his hand is also balanced), he opts for game in no-trumps. He therefore bids the game contract 3NT.

A more specific guide for when to go for game in the three desirable game contracts (3NT, 4♥ and 4♠) is if you and your partner together have 25 points (i.e. ten more than your opponents out of the total, 40). It doesn't guarantee success, and you won't always fail if you have fewer points, but it's a useful guide.

When to go for game

Bidding with your partner involves first trying to find a fit, then seeing whether you have enough points between you for game. This decision process is shown at the top of the page opposite.

must know
- The five game contracts are 3NT, 4♥, 4♠, 5♣ and 5♦.
- Avoid contracts 5♣ and 5♦.
- If you have an opening hand (12+ points) and your partner also has 12+ points, you should contract for game.
- Bid game (3NT, 4♥, 4♠) if your partnership has 25+ points.

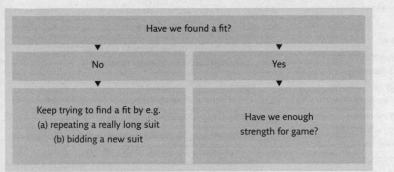

Have we found a fit?	
▼	▼
No	Yes
▼	▼
Keep trying to find a fit by e.g. (a) repeating a really long suit (b) bidding a new suit	Have we enough strength for game?

Now let's look at some sample pairs of hands (we'll assume silence from the opponents). Note that 'responder' is bridge jargon for the opener's partner.

(a)	(b)	(c)
Opener	Opener	Opener
♠ KQ842	♠ AK863	♠ AQJ76
♥ A983	♥ QJ32	♥ KJ76
♦ J9	♦ Q8	♦ 104
♣ K5	♣ 42	♣ J7
Responder	Responder	Responder
♠ AJ63	♠ J742	♠ K4
♥ K5	♥ G4	♥ AQ42
♦ 43	♦ K752	♦ 97
♣ AJ742	♣ K75	♣ A8532

(a) Opener bids 1♠, so responder knows they have at least eight spades between them – a fit. Responder must now bid. There's no point bidding clubs – it would only confuse matters when it's obvious spades should be trumps. The only unresolved issue is how high to bid in spades, specifically whether or not to bid for game (4♠). Responder knows that opener has 12+ points (the minimum required in order to open the bidding), and responder has 13, thus the partnership has at least 25 points, which means that responder can go

must know

Don't bid unnecessarily high when bidding a new suit. Try to find a fit as 'cheaply' as possible i.e. the bid you reach first as you work up the bidding ladder on p. 22 (the bid that requires the least number of tricks to make a contract). Then assess whether or not you have enough points to go for game.

for game: she bids 4♠, a 'jump' from the previous bid 1♠. The bidding sequence is as follows, the underlined bid being the final contract:

Opener	Responder
1♠	<u>4♠</u>
Pass	

(b) Opener bids 1♠. Again responder knows there's a spade fit (opener must have four+ spades, and responder has four spades, so the partnership has eight+ spades). However responder has a relatively low point count, so should raise to 2♠. This conveys to opener that responder supports spades as trumps but her hand is only worth a minimum bid. With nothing to add to his opening bid, opener then passes. They've found their fit but lack the strength for game. The bidding sequence is:

Opener	Responder
1♠	<u>2♠</u>
Pass	

(c) Opener bids 1♠, which doesn't reveal a fit to responder. She therefore tries her favourite (longest) suit at the lowest level possible, bidding 2♣. This suit doesn't appeal to opener, but rather than repeat spades he offers a third choice of trump suit, hearts. Responder now knows they've found their fit (the partnership has at least eight hearts). She considers whether the values for game are present: she has 13 points, and her partner has advertised 12+ by opening, which is enough to bid a game contract (25 points are needed to go for game). Responder jumps to 4♥. The bidding sequence is:

Opener	Responder
1♠	2♣
2♥	<u>4♥</u>
Pass	

Responding to a 1NT opener

If your partner opens the bidding 1NT, as responder you should be happy because he's described his hand very accurately: 12, 13 or 14 points and one of three balanced distributions (see the diagrams on p. 26). In most cases you'll be in a position to place the final contract.

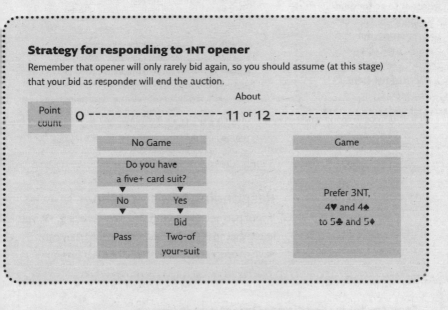

Strategy for responding to 1NT opener

Remember that opener will only rarely bid again, so you should assume (at this stage) that your bid as responder will end the auction.

Point count: 0 ------------------- About 11 or 12 ----------------

No Game
Do you have a five+ card suit?
No → Pass
Yes → Bid Two-of your-suit

Game
Prefer 3NT, 4♥ and 4♠ to 5♣ and 5♦

Now consider how you'd respond to your partner's 1NT opener when you hold the following cards (answers overleaf):

(a)
♠ AJ8
♥ KQ9
♦ K105
♣ J985

(b)
♠ A2
♥ KJ10964
♦ AJ97
♣ 3

(c)
♠ 74
♥ 9853
♦ J9732
♣ 109

must know

- When your partner opens 1NT, as responder you must consider whether to make a trump suit or to stay in no-trumps, and whether to go for game.
- Responding Two-of-a-suit removes your partner's 1NT opener and is known as a 'weakness take-out'.

(a) You know the partnership has enough strength for game (you have 25 or more points between you). With your balanced hand, your preferred bid is 3NT.

(b) You know the values for game are present. You also know there's a heart fit (a 1NT opener can't contain a void or a singleton so your partner must have at least two hearts, which makes at least eight hearts between you). The correct response is jump to 4♥.

(c) With such a weak hand there's clearly no chance of going for game. However, leaving your partner in 1NT would be a mistake so you need to make a bid. Your hand is useless in no-trumps but may take a few tricks with diamonds as trumps, so bid 2♦. Your bid effectively removes your partner's 1NT bid and is known as a 'weakness take-out'. Your partner will know not to bid again (he'll look on your bid as a rescue).

Responding to a suit opener

If your partner opens with One-of-a-suit, e.g. 1♥, you know that 19 is the highest point count they can have to open at this One level (see diagrams on

Strategy for responding to One-of-a-suit opener

If you as responder have six+ points in total then you should keep the bidding open (note the difference between this and responding to 1NT, where the opener's upper limit is 14 points).

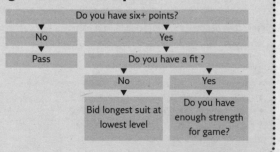

Do you have six+ points?	
No	Yes
Pass	Do you have a fit ?
	No	Yes
	Bid longest suit at lowest level	Do you have enough strength for game?

pp. 29 and 30). This means that you, as responder, need a minimum of six points to have a chance of game (25 points in total are required for game).

Now consider how you should respond to your partner's 1♥ opener if you hold the following cards:

(a)	(b)	(c)
♠ J7	♠ KJ2	♠ KJ732
♥ 85	♥ AQ64	♥ 983
♦ K10532	♦ K963	♦ J932
♣ J985	♣ 32	♣ A

(a) You have fewer than six points. The partnership doesn't hold the 25 points for game, so you should pass. To bid would show (inaccurately) six+ points.

(b) You have plenty of points to respond, plus a fit for hearts. Also, the point count is high enough to go for game (13+12 = 25). You should jump to 4♥.

(c) You easily have enough points to bid, but no guarantee of a fit for hearts (opener may only have four hearts, in which case you'd need four to make the eight required for a fit). Instead you should bid your longest suit at the lowest level, and await developments: a bid of 1♠. This shows you have at least six points in order to bid and at least four spades to try for a fit (see the diagram on p. 31), and, by inference, you have fewer than four hearts.

must know
• The responder to a One-of-suit opener should bid if she has six+ points in her hand, and pass if she has fewer points than this.
• The opener of One-of-a-suit must bid again if his partner bids a different suit.

Bidding after an opponent's opener

If you bid (or 'call') after the opponents have opened the bidding then you are 'overcalling'.

Overcalling

Unlike opening, you don't need 12 points to enter the bidding when overcalling, but you should only enter the bidding for a reason, i.e. when you have strong

must know

• An overcall in a suit indicates five+ decent cards in the suit.

• An overcall doesn't guarantee that the overcaller has opening points (12 or more), but equally it doesn't preclude them.

cards in a long suit. Sometimes you may be able to steal the contract from your opponents, or you may simply be aiming to cause them trouble by using up their bidding space (their opportunities to communicate with each other) or pushing them to make an unwise bid at too high a level.

The crucial difference in bidding an overcall is that where an opening bid and response only promise a minimum of four cards in the bid suit, an overcall guarantees a minimum of five cards. The corollary to this is that the overcaller's partner only needs a three-card support to make the fit of eight cards (see the figure below).

4+ cards to support partner
4+ cards to bid a suit
6+ points to respond

Responder

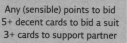

Any (sensible) points to bid
5+ decent cards to bid a suit
3+ cards to support partner

Any (sensible) points to bid
5+ decent cards to bid a suit
3+ cards to support partner

Opener

12+ points to open (at One level)
4+ cards to bid a suit
4+ cards to support partner

Note that both members of the overcalling side adhere to the same guidelines – it doesn't matter if you're bidding directly over an opening bid, or over the response.

Here are three sample hands that would make a 1♠ overcall following your opponents' opening bid of 1♥ (or after the bidding sequence: 1♣, Pass, 1♥).

(a)	(b)	(c)
♠ AQ1074	♠ KQ952	♠ AKJ74
♥ 85	♥ 10864	♥ 983
♦ Q1092	♦ A63	♦ A
♣ 75	♣ 2	♣ J874

(a) and (b) are not particularly strong hands, but there's everything to be gained by mentioning your spades in each case: it's the highest-ranked suit (see pp. 8 and 22) and you may go on to make a contract. Even if it's just a case of disrupting your opponents' bidding, and ultimately defending, you'll have helped your partner's defence by indicating which suit to lead.

(c) is another clear overcall of 1♠. Note that an overcall is possible with opening bid values (12+ points).

Doubling

The final bid in the bridge player's arsenal is a double. When you bid 'Double' literally this means that you double the opposing contract because you think it will fail, and if you're right you get more points for your side. However, the most frequent use for the double is something quite different: to ask your partner to bid in one of the unbid suits.

We'll talk much more about the double in chapter 4 (see p. 126). For now, accept that the following hands (a, b and c) would double a 1♥ opener from the opposition:

(a)	(b)	(c)
♠ KJ97	♠ AKJ	♠ Q987
♥ 85	♥ 10	♥ A3
♦ AQ3	♦ Q9763	♦ A952
♣ Q1065	♣ KJ75	♣ AKQ

must know

If you bid 'Double' following an opening suit bid from the opposition this normally indicates you have an opening hand (12+ points) supporting all unbid suits, and it implicitly asks your partner to bid one of these other suits.

Play

Once the bidding has finished, as declarer you now need to make the required number of tricks to achieve your contract, or as a defender you need to stop declarer from doing this.

Playing our first deal in no-trumps

When there is no trump suit, in each round of play the highest card in the lead suit wins the trick. A player unable to follow suit cannot win the trick so must throw away a card in a different suit.

As declarer you must plan your strategy before you play from dummy at Trick one. First count how many tricks are 'off the top', i.e. how many you can make before losing the lead. Note that you don't play out these 'top tricks' at this stage.

Let's return to a previous example:

North (dummy)	South (declarer)
♠ AQJ2	♠ K3
♥ K4	♥ A52
♦ Q1052	♦ KJ43
♣ J75	♣ Q832

Between the two hands, declarer has four top spades (provided he plays his top cards in the right order) and two top hearts: a total of six. Note that he doesn't have any top tricks in diamonds and clubs – he'll have to lose the lead before establishing tricks in these suits. In the bidding he has contracted for 3NT (six plus three = nine tricks out of a total of 13) and he can now work out that he needs three extra tricks to win (six + three extra = nine). He has two options:

(a) To take the six top tricks (i.e. ♠AKQJ and ♥AK) straight away, then look around for the three more he needs. (b) To focus first on generating those three extra tricks. The wisest strategy on almost all deals (and particularly no-trumps) is (b). The two strategies can be likened to a tortoise and a hare.

Tortoise and hare

I often equate the choice of strategies in a bridge deal to a race between a tortoise and a hare. The hare loves to get off to a flying start; cashing his top tricks straight away. The tortoise, on the other hand, is happy to lose the lead early, knowing he'll polish up later on.

In the example on p. 40, let's see what happens to the hare. He cashes all his spades and hearts, then, unable to cash any more tricks, turns to diamonds. The difficulties arise because when his opponents win the lead – as they're sure to with ♦A – they'll go on to cash promoted low-card winners in hearts (and perhaps spades) with cards left over in their hands. Together with ♦A and ♣AK (tricks he has no choice but to lose), the hare will lose too many tricks and fail to make his contract. There's no bonus for taking early tricks.

The tortoise, on the other hand, wins ♥K, then focuses on establishing the three extra tricks (additional to his six top tricks) needed for his nine-trick contract. He works out that these can all be made by forcing out ♦A. At trick two, he leads ♦Q (he could equally well lead ♦10, or ♦2 to ♦K/♦J). His opponents are likely to win ♦A on this trick; if they don't, the tortoise's ♦Q is promoted into a trick and he leads a second diamond to force out ♦A. The beauty of flushing out ♦A early on is that the tortoise retains control of the other suits. If his opponents decide to cash ♣A and ♣K, this will promote the tortoise's ♣Q and ♣J. More likely, they'll lead a second heart. The tortoise then wins ♥A and has three promoted diamond winners. All he needs to do is cash his four top spades without blocking himself, to give him his nine top tricks. He plays ♠K first (highest card from the shorter length) and leads ♠3 to ♠AQJ. Nine tricks and game contract made.

Useful tip

You defend half of all contracts, and only declare a quarter of them, so learn to love defence – it's a wonderful co-operative challenge.

Defending

You didn't win the bidding and are defending. Here are some strategies you should adopt:

Opening lead

The opening lead is unique. It's the only card you as defenders play without sight of dummy's hand, as the lead card is always played by the player on declarer's left before dummy tables her cards. Because the opening lead is a bit like a stab in the dark, you should stick to tried-and-tested ploys. Much depends on whether you're defending against a trump or no-trump contract.

Defending against no-trumps

Against no-trumps, you should focus on length. If you can exhaust declarer and dummy of their cards in your longest suit, you'll have small cards left over and these will be length winners. Your opening lead should therefore be a low card from your longest suit, or from your partner's if she has bid.

Defending against trumps

The length strategy is far less powerful against a trump contract as declarer will simply trump you when he's run out of cards in the lead suit. At the other end of the spectrum, leading a singleton (in a 'side suit', i.e. not trumps) is a powerful ploy. You can void yourself (run out of cards in the suit) in the hope that the suit will be played again and you can trump.

More common than the singleton is the 'top-of-a-sequence' lead: when defending against a trump contract, and you hold two or more high cards in a sequence (known as 'touching' high cards), lead with the top card in the sequence. For example, if you hold the ace and king in a suit, then it's standard practice to lead with the ace; if you hold the king and queen, then lead the king; if you hold the queen and jack, lead the queen; if you hold the jack and ten, lead the jack; or lead the ten if you hold ten and nine. Thus, if you lead with the king and hold the queen, this puts you in a win-win position: your partner may hold the ace, in which case your king will win the trick; and even if the declarer or dummy takes the king with the ace you'll have promoted your queen into a second-round winner.

After the lead

As you begin bridge, you'll probably find defending to be the toughest part of the game. Your instinct may well be to throw down an ace or two, grabbing tricks quickly. This wasn't the right strategy for the declarer (remember the hare), and nor is it the right strategy for defence. An ace is meant to catch a king, and not two low cards, as it is sure to do if you use it hastily.

Here are three of the most important factors to bear in mind when defending:

Trick target
Never lose sight of how many tricks you need to defeat the contract and stop your opponents scoring points towards a game (see pp. 221–2).

Observe dummy
Look for dummy's weakest suit – e.g. one with three small cards.

Partner
Work out what kind of hand your partner holds: did she bid? What did she lead? Why did she lead what she led?

To remember this, 'TOP' stands for 'Trick target', 'Observe dummy' and 'Partner'.

want to know more?
• The system of bidding assumed in this book is the English Standard 'Acol', the most prevalent in Britain. For more on different bidding systems, see p. 231.
• For more ways to make tricks, see pp. 78–89.
• For playing a deal in a trump suit, see pp. 84–9.
• For more on the opening lead and defence, see pp. 90–103.

Three basic deals

You may find it helpful to lay out all 52 cards and play through the following illustrative deals with open cards. When each card is played, turn it face down beside the hand, vertically if won by the partnership, and horizontally if lost.

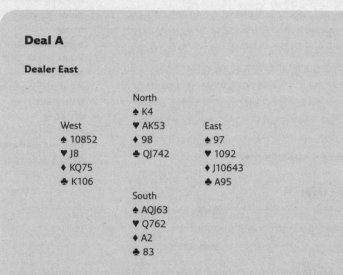

Deal A

Dealer East

```
                      North
                      ♠ K4
                      ♥ AK53
      West            ♦ 98           East
      ♠ 10852         ♣ QJ742        ♠ 97
      ♥ J8                           ♥ 1092
      ♦ KQ75                         ♦ J10643
      ♣ K106                         ♣ A95
                      South
                      ♠ AQJ63
                      ♥ Q762
                      ♦ A2
                      ♣ 83
```

The bidding:

East deals, so is first to speak. Lacking 12 points, he says 'No Bid'. The bidding moves clockwise to South, who, since the bidding has not yet been opened, also needs (at least) 12 points to bid. He has them. He opens One of his Longest Suit, One Spade. West passes – although he does not need 12 points to bid (now that the bidding has been opened), he should have a nice five-card suit (which he does not have). North can work out that the points for game (25) are present between the partnership. But there is no rush – for he does not know the trump suit. He simply bids his longest suit at the lowest level – Two Clubs – and awaits developments.

With East-West silent, South then considers what to do next. He knows that his partner does not particularly like his spades (no support); and he does not like his partner's clubs. Rather than sing the same song twice and repeat the spades, he suggests a new alternative, hearts, knowing that his partner will realize he prefers spades – because he bid them first. Over his bid of Two Hearts, North perks up. The fit is found – South must have four+ hearts, giving a partnership total of the magic eight. It was not the first-choice trump suit for either player, but together, hearts are best.

It's like partners in life: 'I want to watch the football tonight.' 'Oh, I'd like to go to the movies.' Eventually the two go out and have a meal together – neither of their first choices. But the best combined option – and delicious!

The one remaining issue is whether or not to go for game. Because North knows that the points for game (25) are present (he has 13 and his partner opened the bidding to indicate at least 12), the answer to that question is 'yes'. North jumps to Four Hearts. Everybody passes – end of the bidding.

Here is the bidding sequence in full:

East	South	West	North
Pass	1♠	Pass	2♣
Pass	2♥	Pass	4♥
Pass	Pass	Pass	

The play:

By bidding the trump suit – hearts – first, South is declarer. West (on South's left) must make the opening lead, after which North lays out his cards (for he is dummy).

West has heard his opponents bid all the suits bar diamonds. This makes diamonds an intelligent choice of opening lead, likely to hit their weakness. Leading diamonds is still more attractive because West holds a king-queen combination in the suit. He leads the king of diamonds (top-of-a-sequence – indicating the queen), and will be very happy to see it win the trick (should his partner hold the ace), but almost as happy seeing it force out the ace and so promote his queen.

Declarer wins the ace of diamonds, and looks at his lovely spades. Before he can enjoy them (without the risk of them being trumped), he must get rid of ('draw') the opposing trumps. Because he has eight trumps, he can work out that the opponents hold five. He expects those five missing trumps to split three-two, in which case they will all be gone in three rounds. It does not matter in which order he plays his three top cards, so say that at Trick Two he leads to dummy's king. When both opponents follow, he knows there are three trumps left out. He follows with dummy's ace of trumps and, with both opponents following a second time (good!), he now knows that the opposing trumps have indeed split three-two. There is just one trump outstanding. If it was higher than all of his remaining trumps, he would leave it out. Because it is lower, however, he leads to his queen to get rid of it. Trumps have now been drawn, and note the method of counting (focusing only on the missing cards and counting down). It would be a bad move to lead out the fourth round of trumps - wasting the two small trumps together. Play correctly, and declarer will make those trumps separately - let's see how.

The opposing trumps drawn, declarer now turns his attention to spades. Following the unblocking principle of leading the highest card from the shorter length first when holding sequential high cards between the two hands, at Trick Five declarer leads a low spade to dummy's king. He returns a second spade to his jack, and then cashes the ace. He has the opportunity to make a discard from dummy on this trick - can you spot the best play? Declarer can get rid of dummy's remaining diamond. He next cashes the queen of spades, discarding a club from dummy. Say he has been counting the six missing spades as they fall (although my recommendation at this juncture is to limit yourself to counting one suit per deal - here that suit being trumps - so don't feel a failure if the idea of having to count spades too fills you with horror); he will then know that all the opposing spades have gone. He leads his fifth-round six of spades, and it is a length winner. Rather than trump it, he discards another club.

Here is the position, with declarer on lead having won the first nine tricks, and everybody left with four cards:

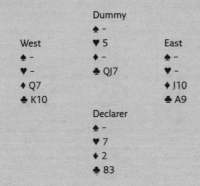

Dummy
♠ -
♥ 5
♦ -
♣ QJ7

West
♠ -
♥ -
♦ Q7
♣ K10

East
♠ -
♥ -
♦ J10
♣ A9

Declarer
♠ -
♥ 7
♦ 2
♣ 83

Declarer could simply lead out his last trump and secure his ten-trick game. But making overtricks counts extra points (albeit 'above the line' – see chapter 5: Scoring), so instead he leads the two of diamonds, trumping it in dummy with the five of trumps. At this juncture he has to lead a club, enabling the opponents to win their ace-king of the suit. But the last trick is taken by declarer's remaining trump, and he has made a total of 11 tricks. Note how he scored the two remaining trumps separately.

Game made – with an overtrick.

If you remember just one thing about ...

Bidding: Bid new suits at the lowest level (provided at least four cards are held), until a fit is found.

Declaring: When counting a suit (say trumps), work out how many cards are missing, and count down those missing cards, preferably thinking in terms of their likely split.

Defending: The lead of a high card (such as West's king of diamonds) is normally top-of-a-sequence of two or more. Thus partner knows both that you have the card immediately below, and that you deny the one immediately above.

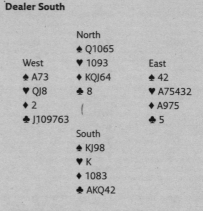

Deal B

Dealer South

```
                North
                ♠ Q1065
West            ♥ 1093          East
♠ A73           ♦ KQJ64         ♠ 42
♥ QJ8           ♣ 8             ♥ A75432
♦ 2                             ♦ A975
♣ J109763                       ♣ 5
                South
                ♠ KJ98
                ♥ K
                ♦ 1083
                ♣ AKQ42
```

The bidding:

South deals the cards and opens the bidding –
One Club. West passes – although he does not
need 12 points now that the bidding has already
been opened, the one suit worth mentioning has
been bid by an opponent, and it can't be right for
both sides to be bidding the same suit. North
hates clubs, so bids his longest suit at the lowest
level – in a fit-finding exercise. After North's bid of
One Diamond, East offers One Heart. His lack of
points is more than made up for by his long heart
suit and interesting shape. Back to South – who
must bid One Spade. Why?

South does not know that his partner has a fifth
diamond – and whether there is a fit. Furthermore,
a fit in a major suit (spades or hearts) is more
valuable than a fit in a minor suit (diamonds or
clubs). This is because 11 tricks need to be made
in order to score game (5♦/5♣), whereas only ten
are required to make game in a major (4♠/4♥). So
South must try One Spade – perhaps there is a fit

good to know
Do not bid a suit that
an opponent has bid.

there. He must never forget that North knows that clubs is his first-choice trump suit, as he bid them first.

Over to West, who has heard his partner overcall One Heart, indicating five+ hearts. With three-card support, West knows that his side has an eight-card fit. He bids Two Hearts. Now North. He has four-card support for partner's spades (making a fit) so bids Two Spades. East would much rather make hearts trumps – even at the cost of needing to make nine tricks, so competes with Three Hearts. It pays to be bold with a fit, and South, using the same logic, competes to Three Spades. Everybody now passes – having bid their cards to the full.

Here is the bidding sequence:

South	West	North	East
1♣	Pass	1♦	1♥
1♠	2♥	2♠	3♥
3♠	Pass	Pass	Pass

The play:

By bidding spades first, South becomes declarer (*he will do this a lot in written deals – for the simple reason that it is easier to orient yourself as declarer when in the South position*). West must make the opening lead, and has two good choices. He could lead the suit his side has bid and supported, hearts, and would select the queen (top of a sequence – showing the jack); alternatively, he could lead his singleton diamond, in the hope of using his trumps to trump later rounds of diamonds. Which way to go?

It is one of the beautiful uncertainties of the game that some days one choice will work out better; other days the opposite applies. But I'd probably opt for the singleton. Such a lead can be spectacularly

good to know
It pays to be bold
when you have a fit.

successful, and, furthermore, West knows that he can win the first round of trumps, preventing declarer from drawing his trumps and avoiding the threat of him trumping a diamond. West leads the two of diamonds.

Can East interpret the lead correctly? He wins the ace of diamonds, and reflects that West must have a good reason not to lead hearts – the suit East bid. That reason must be that his diamond was a singleton. East promptly leads back a second diamond at Trick Two. Bingo! West trumps it. At Trick Three West switches to the queen of hearts in an attempt to put his partner on play. The lead of the queen (top of a high-card sequence) denies the king, so East plays the ace. Note that even though his partner is currently winning the trick, East knows that declarer has the king, and will win the trick unless East plays the ace. His ace fells declarer's king (you can see that East would have 'gone to bed' with his ace if he had not played it at this juncture). At Trick Four East returns another diamond, and West trumps again. His ace of trumps is bound to take the setting trick.

Although play continues until the end, declarer can make all bar that ace of trumps by playing trumps, losing to the ace, drawing East's second trump, then playing club and diamond winners. Eight tricks made, against nine bid. Down one.

Everybody is happy with this result. East-West are happy because they defeated South's Three Spade contract. But North-South are also happy – for East would almost certainly have made Three Hearts, and it is much better to go down one than let the opponents make a contract. Points below the line (resulting from a making contract – and counting towards game) are far more valuable than points above the line which do not count towards game (see chapter 5: Scoring). Hence the expression 'Down one is good Bridge!'.

If you remember just one thing about ...

Bidding: Try to declare when both sides have a fit. Even if you go down one in your contract, it is preferable to letting the opponents make their contract.

Declaring: Play carefully to the bitter end, even if you are already down. Loss limitation is an important part of the game.

Defending: If partner makes an unexpected play (e.g. West's failure to lead a heart), he should have a good reason (here West's diamond is bound to be a singleton).

Deal C

Dealer South

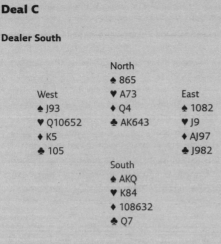

```
                    North
                    ♠ 865
        West        ♥ A73        East
        ♠ J93       ♦ Q4         ♠ 1082
        ♥ Q10652    ♣ AK643      ♥ J9
        ♦ K5                     ♦ AJ97
        ♣ 105                    ♣ J982
                    South
                    ♠ AKQ
                    ♥ K84
                    ♦ 108632
                    ♣ Q7
```

The bidding:

South has a balanced hand (5332) with 12-14 points: perfect for a One No-trump opener. West passes: to overcall at the Two-level requires much more, both in the way of points, and strength of suit. North knows that his partnership has the values for game – but which one? Game in clubs is two more tricks than game in no-trumps, so North makes the clear-cut bid of Three No-trumps (mistaken even to mention clubs, as you know what the final contract should be).

The sequence has been brief but effective (the fewer the bids, the less chance to go wrong!):

South	West	North	East
1NT	Pass	3NT	Pass
Pass	Pass		

The play:

The defence must focus on length against a no-trump contract, so West leads a low heart. Declaring a no-trump contract, it is particularly imperative that declarer starts by counting up his 'top' tricks – the ones he can make before losing the lead. He is not going to play them all out –

like our hare – but he needs to see how many extra tricks he must make. Looking at dummy's holding in conjunction with his own in each suit, he counts three top tricks in spades, two in hearts, and three in clubs: total eight. He needs one more, and the length in the clubs offers by far the best chance. He will need to count the opponents' clubs as they fall, but he notes that they begin with six clubs.

Declarer plays a low heart from dummy, and beats East's jack with his king. Focusing on clubs, he cashes the queen first (high card from the shorter length), and leads a club to dummy's king. Both follow suit twice, but when he next leads the ace of clubs (discarding a heart from his hand), West also discards (a spade). Had both opponents followed a third time, meaning that clubs had split three-three, dummy's two remaining clubs would be length winners. But they did not – instead splitting four-two. Should he abandon clubs?

Absolutely not – you have lose to win in bridge. Declarer leads a fourth club from dummy, losing the trick to East's jack (and throwing a diamond from his hand, as West sheds another spade). If the defenders could see each other's hands, East would switch to a low diamond at this point, enabling them to win the king, then the ace (taking dummy's queen), then the jack; but this would not defeat declarer as he would have the fourth round master with the ten. In practice, East is likely to return his partner's hearts. Declarer wins dummy's ace (note how important it was that declarer saved this card, as a way of getting back to dummy), and can now proudly lead the promoted fifth-round length winner in clubs. This is his extra trick, and now he can play like a hare, grabbing the ace-king-queen of spades, to bring his trick tally to nine. Game made.

If you remember just one thing about ...

Bidding: Do not look for minor-suit games.
Declaring: Count your top tricks before embarking. Immediately look for the extra ones.
Defending: Lead from your longest suit against a no-trump contract.

3 Core

You've learnt the basics and it's time to consider the game in detail. Work your way through this chapter and you'll be playing intermediate-level bridge. There's more on bidding (opening, responding and overcalling), and on play (cashing tricks and defending). Before embarking on this core section, make sure you have a game or two – there's no substitute for playing. Get a feel for what bridge is about: describing your cards to your partner during the bidding, then taking as many tricks as possible during the play.

More on bidding

As we've seen, the first job in bidding is to find a trump fit; the second is to decide how many tricks to aim for, and whether to go for game. With experience you'll find that an active style – grabbing any opportunity to show your partner your best (longest) suit – is a winning one.

must know

The Rule of 20 (when to open): add the points in your hand to the number of cards in your two longest suits. If the total reaches 20 or more, you should open the bidding. The Rule of 20 only applies to unbalanced hands.

Opening the bidding

Up to now we've been working on the basis that you need 12 points to open the bidding (at the One level). Now we'll look at a case where you can open with less: when you have an interesting distribution.

Here are three examples of One-level opening hands that contain fewer than 12 points:

(a)	(b)	(c)
♠ 8	♠ A972	♠ KJ943
♥ KQ9742	♥ 64	♥ 98
♦ K105	♦ AQ9732	♦ AQ732
♣ K85	♣ 3	♣ 9

Note that all three hands are unbalanced (all three have a singleton). If you follow the Rule of 20 you can open the bidding with all three. With (a) you can open 1♥, and with (b) you can open 1♦. With hand (c) you have two equal-length suits: we'll consider which suit to open shortly (see pp. 56–7).

Once you know you have enough points to open the bidding (or satisfy the Rule of 20), you must check whether your hand is balanced or unbalanced as your bidding strategy depends on this. To remind you, a balanced hand contains no void, no singleton and not more than one doubleton.

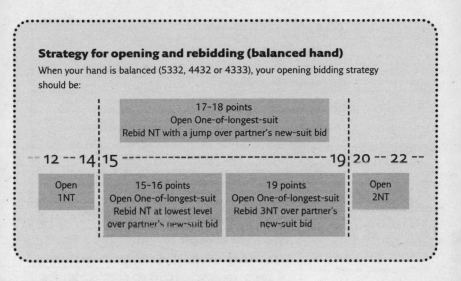

Strategy for opening and rebidding (balanced hand)

When your hand is balanced (5332, 4432 or 4333), your opening bidding strategy should be:

		17–18 points Open One-of-longest-suit Rebid NT with a jump over partner's new-suit bid		
— 12 — 14	15	—————————————————————	19	20 — 22 —
Open 1NT	15–16 points Open One-of-longest-suit Rebid NT at lowest level over partner's new-suit bid	19 points Open One-of-longest-suit Rebid 3NT over partner's new-suit bid		Open 2NT

Let's consider the bidding strategies for the following balanced hands:

(a)	(b)	(c)
♠ 63	♠ 98752	♠ AJ
♥ KJ742	♥ Q3	♥ QJ97
♦ AQ5	♦ AKQ	♦ QJ2
♣ K85	♣ AJ10	♣ AK105

(a) Open 1NT. Even with a five-card major, 1NT is more accurately descriptive of your hand than 1♥. And opening 1NT means you don't have to bid again – and normally won't. If you open One-of-a-suit, however, you must bid again if your partner changes the suit.

(b) Open 1♠. With 15 points you must open One-of-a-suit (too many points for 1NT) and show the balanced nature of your hand by rebidding no-trumps next time (at the lowest level over your partner's new-suit bid).

(c) Open 1♣/♥ (we'll discuss which shortly). With 18 points you should open One-of-a-suit, planning to rebid 2NT (jumping up a level) over your partner's new-suit bid, of, say, 1♠.

Opening bid summary

- When opening, first count your points and check if your hand is balanced or unbalanced.
- If you can open 1NT (because you have a balanced hand with 12–14 points), then you always should.
- If you have too many points (15 or more) to open 1NT, but have a balanced opening hand, plan to bid no-trumps with your second bid. (Don't do this with an unbalanced opening hand.)
- If you have an unbalanced hand and satisfy the Rule of 20 (see p. 54), then you should open the bidding with One-of-a-suit.

Which suit to open?

Let's assume your point count falls outside the 12–14 (or 20–22) range so you can't open 1NT (or 2NT). You now have to choose an opening suit. If you have one suit longer than the others, then this is the obvious choice – even if it's weak in high cards (the longer a suit, the more desirable a trump suit it will make). However, if you have two (or more) equal-length suits, I recommend the tried-and-tested approach of opening with the higher-ranking of the two. This favours the major suits (spades and hearts), which score more points.

There's just one exception: when you hold precisely four spades and four hearts (and can't open 1NT or 2NT), you should open 1♥ (even though it ranks lower than 1♠). This gives the partnership the maximum chance of finding a major-suit fit as it allows your partner to support hearts or respond in spades at the One level. If you open 1♠, on the other hand, you may miss a heart fit if your partner feels that her hand is not strong enough to bid hearts at the Two level.

see p. 54

must know

If you can open 1NT (i.e. you have a balanced hand and 12–14 points) then you must. There's no later bid that says, 'Partner, I forgot to open 1NT last time'. For example, if you opened 1♣, then rebid 1NT over your partner's 1♥, you'd be saying to your partner you have a balanced hand with 15–16 points – very misleading if you have only 12–14 points.

Now try choosing an opening bid for the following hands:

(a)	(b)	(c)	(d)	(e)
♠ 8	♠ Q4	♠ J109642	♠ AQ53	♠ KJ976
♥ 109532	♥ KQ64	♥ Q32	♥ K1095	♥ AQ1087
♦ AKQ8	♦ KJ86	♦ A	♦ A64	♦ 97
♣ Q105	♣ A107	♣ A95	♣ Q9	♣ 10

(a) Open 1♥. You have an unbalanced hand and just eleven points but can open using the Rule of 20. Open in the longest suit, not the strongest.

(b) Open 1♥, the higher ranking of two equal-length suits. If your partner responds with, say, 1♠, your rebid should be 1NT (indicating 15–16 points and a balanced hand).

(c) Open 1♠ (Rule of 20), and plan to repeat the spades with your rebid.

(d) Open 1♥. With four-four lengths in both majors, the only exception to the 'open higher ranking of equal-length suits' guideline applies: open the cheaper suit.

(e) Open 1♠. Another Rule-of-20 opener. With equal-length suits in the majors, but five-five instead of four-four lengths, open the higher ranking of the two suits.

must know
• With one suit longer than all others, open that suit.
• With two equally long suits, open the higher-ranking.
• The only exception is the 'open the higher-ranking of two equal length suits' guideline. This occurs with precisely four-four in the majors (open 1♥). By opening the cheaper suit you make finding a fit easier.

Opener's rebid

Your second bid ('rebid') after opening, following a
change-of-suit by your partner, is always linked to
your opening bid. As we've already seen, if you have
a balanced hand but too many points to open no-
trumps, you should plan to rebid no-trumps at your
second bid (see p. 55). But what if you have an
unbalanced hand?

Look at hands (a), (b) and (c) below – three
typical unbalanced opening hands. These
represent the most common unbalanced shapes: a
'five-four', a 'six-card suit' and (somewhat less
likely) a 'five-five'.

What should the rebids be, assuming your partner makes a
change-of-suit response to your opener?

(a)	(b)	(c)
♠ 8	♠ J109642	♠ KJ976
♥ 109532	♥ Q32	♥ AQ1087
♦ AKQ8	♦ A	♦ 97
♣ Q105	♣ A95	♣ 10

(a) Open 1♥ and rebid 2♦. Although the 1♥ opener guarantees
a minimum of four cards, when you introduce a second suit
you're saying you have at least five hearts. Put another way,
you wouldn't bid a second suit unless you had (at least) five
cards in your first. (Note this would exclude the troublesome
but less common shape of 4441.)

(b) Open 1♠, then repeat your spades in the rebid. To repeat
a suit strongly implies (if not guarantees) six+ cards (rather
than five).

(c) Having correctly opened 1♠, you should follow with hearts.
Note that the auction 1♠-2♣-2♥ would allow your partner the
opportunity to revert to your first suit at the Two level (i.e. 2♠),
whereas 1♥-2♣-2♠ would force her to a less economical Three-
level bid if she wanted to revert to your first suit.

Responding to a 1NT opener

We had our first look at responding to your partner's 1NT opener on p. 35. It is now time to take things a step further, and add more definition and accuracy.

Which zone?

As responder you must assess in which 'zone' the partnership lies: part-score or game (or slam – see chapter 4). A part-score is a contract that doesn't give game in one deal, but two or more part-scores may add up to game over several deals (see p. 221 for more on scoring part-scores and games). First add up your hand's point score, then use the following guidelines to determine your zone and appropriate response.

Part-score

With ten points or fewer, the values for game aren't present and you must settle in the best (least bad) part-score. If you have a long suit (at least five cards) you should respond to your partner's 1NT opener with a Two-level bid in your long suit. Having the long suit as trumps will more than compensate having to make one extra trick. If you don't have a long suit, you have little choice but to pass.

Part-score/game

With 11 or 12 points, you're in the 'game-invitational zone' where you need to ask your partner if he wishes to play a game contract or to settle for a (safer) part-score. Because of the limitations of the bidding code, there's only one invitational response to a 1NT opener – 2NT – to which your partner can accept the invitation to game (bid 3NT) or reject it (pass). Note that the 2NT invitation only aims for a game in no-trumps so isn't appropriate for many unbalanced and major-suited hands. On these occasions, you (responder) must decide alone whether to settle for the part-score (with a Two-bid of your longest suit), or whether to force to game.

Game

With 13+ points, you're in the 'game zone' and it's just a question of finding the right game. The game contracts, as we've seen, are 3NT, 4♥, 4♠, 5♣ and 5♦. Avoid 5♣ and 5♦: having to make two more tricks than with 3NT can be difficult. The best strategy with a minor-suited hand is simply to jump to 3NT. However, 4♥ and 4♠ (each requiring one more trick than 3NT) are usually easier to make than 3NT when the partnership holds eight hearts or eight spades. If you (responder) hold a six-card major suit, you know you have a fit (the 1NT opener must hold at least a doubleton) so you can jump to 4♥/♠. With five cards, however, you can't be certain of a fit so in this case make a Three-level bid of your major suit, which offers your partner (opener) a choice of games: 3NT or 4♥/♠.

> **must know**
> The highest priority game contracts are 4♥ and 4♠ when an eight-card fit is held.

Let's consider the best response to your partner's 1NT opener with each of the following hands:

(a)	(b)	(c)	(d)	(e)	(f)
♠ KJ10876	♠ A62	♠ AQ962	♠ 95	♠ 976	♠ 8632
♥ Q102	♥ 106	♥ J	♥ K852	♥ J6	♥ A7
♦ 9	♦ AK753	♦ AJ103	♦ 97653	♦ K6	♦ K642
♣ AQ5	♣ 876	♣ 864	♣ 64	♣ AKQ987	♣ K42

(a) Bid game contract 4♠. You have the values for game (or at most one point short but the length of the spades and overall shape will compensate). Plus you have a definite eight-card spade fit.

(b) Invitational bid 2NT. This shows 11-12 points and a balanced hand. Opener will then raise to 3NT if he has 14 points (or a promising-looking 13), or pass with 12 points (or a poor-looking 13).

(c) Bid 3♠. This shows a game-going hand with precisely five spades. Opener will then raise to 4♠ if he has three+ spades, or otherwise bid 3NT.

(d) Bid 2♦. This is a 'weakness take out' (see p. 36). Opener will always pass, as you could have no points at all.

(e) Bid 3NT. Don't bother to bid clubs (even 3♣). 3NT – two tricks fewer to make than 5♣ – is almost bound to be an easier game contract.

(f) Pass. Although you have a useful hand, you know (because your partner's maximum point count is 14) that you don't quite have the values for game. Note that you never bid to increase the size of the part-score. Bidding 2NT would invite your partner to bid 3NT – and you don't want that.

Note that in examples (a), (d), (e) and (f), you (as responder) select the final contract.

Rebid by 1NT opener

There are only two occasions when you (as the 1NT opener) will be asked to look at your hand again:

(i) When responder makes an invitational response of 2NT. When this happens, your rebid should be as follows: with a minimum (12-point) hand you should pass, with a maximum (14-point) hand you should bid game contract 3NT, or with a medium (13-point) hand you should go for game if you have a five+ card suit and/or tens and nines.

(ii) When responder jumps to 3♥ or 3♠, showing she has precisely five of that major and a game-going hand. In this case, you should raise to 4♥/♠ if you have three or more cards in support, or rebid 3NT if you have a doubleton. Note that you should not pass: responder has announced game values by jumping to 3♥/♠, but these bids don't give game so it's up to you, the opener, to make a bid that reaches game. The next diagram shows the bids that reach game (the 'game line') – 100 points are needed for game (see chapter 5 for more on scoring).

must know
All bids are either 'forcing' (i.e. forcing a further bid from your partner) or 'non-forcing' (i.e. your partner can pass). Responder's jump to 3♥/♠ over a 1NT opener is forcing.

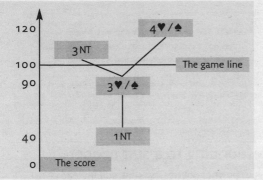

Now consider when you should accept your partner's game invitation in the examples below. In each case you open 1NT and your partner raises to 2NT, inviting you to game. Remember, you'd accept the invitation with 14 points (your maximum) and reject it with 12. The hands shown each contain 13 points – you need to work out which are 'good' 13 point counts and which are 'bad'.

(a)	(b)	(c)
♠ 63	♠ Q32	♠ J10
♥ A97	♥ J742	♥ Q1095
♦ QJ1095	♦ KJ6	♦ KJ108
♣ AQ8	♣ AQ8	♣ AQ8

(a) Good – bid 3NT. You have excellent diamonds: a great use of just three points. This sequential five-card suit is bound to provide a trick source.

(b) Bad – pass. Making even eight tricks will be a struggle here. You have the worst shape: just one four-card suit (a poor one) from which to make length winners. None of your honours (ace, king, queen, jack and ten) are in sequence (again, this would make trick-taking easier), and you have no tens or nines (these don't count points but are

Useful tip
Bridge is ultimately a game about taking tricks, not about high-card points. The more experienced you become, the less you'll rely on high-card point strictures.

must know

Don't bid to increase
the size of the part-
score. Only bid on if
you're interested in
game, or want to
change the trump suit.

useful). The jam is too thinly spread. Much
better to have a trick source (diamonds), even at
the cost of a weakness (spades) – see hand (a).

(c) Good – bid 3NT. Look at those fabulous
intermediate cards.

Responding to a suit opener

If your partner opens One-of-a-suit instead of 1NT,
this shows he has either a balanced hand and 15–19
points, or an unbalanced hand and 12–19 points (see
the diagram below). In case he holds the maximum
point count for this opener (19 points) you as
responder must keep the bidding open if you have
six+ points – added to your partner's points you'd
have enough for game. With fewer than six points,
you should pass.

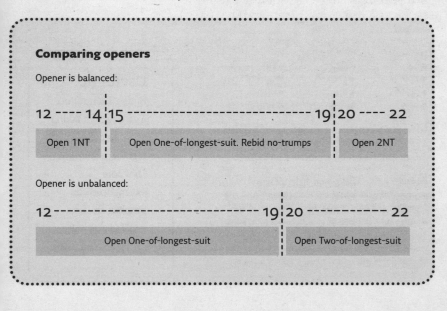

Comparing openers

Opener is balanced:

12 ---- 14	15 ----------------------------- 19	20 ---- 22
Open 1NT	Open One-of-longest-suit. Rebid no-trumps	Open 2NT

Opener is unbalanced:

12 ------------------------------------- 19	20 ----------- 22
Open One-of-longest-suit	Open Two-of-longest-suit

Responder's support line

Once you know you have enough points to keep the bidding open, your job is to find a trump fit. If you (responder) hold four cards in your partner's opening suit, thereby revealing a fit, you must support your partner's bid by raising the bid level. How much to bid depends on your strength. The principle is simple: the more you bid the better your hand. Raising One to Two shows the weakest hand (six points or a little more), while raising One to Four (game in a major suit) shows a guaranteed 25 points (with your partner having advertised 12+ points for his opening bid, you'd need 13+ for this). Your bidding options are shown in the 'Responder's Support Line' below.

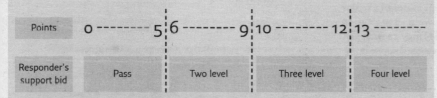

Points	0 -------- 5	6 -------- 9	10 -------- 12	13 --------
Responder's support bid	Pass	Two level	Three level	Four level

NB: Be prepared to upgrade your bid to a higher level than indicated by points alone if you have an interesting distribution, e.g. singletons and voids in suits that are not trumps mean you can easily trump when that suit is played out (see p. 42 and methods for evaluating a bridge hand on pp. 190–5).

Let's consider what you should bid in response to your partner's 1♠ opener with the following hands:

(a)	(b)	(c)
♠ KJ75	♠ A972	♠ QJ84
♥ Q2	♥ 4	♥ A8
♦ K1053	♦ J10932	♦ AQ732
♣ Q85	♣ 752	♣ 94

(a) Bid 3♠. This shows you have four+ spades and 10–12 points.

must know

• Support your partner's opening bid if you have at least four-card support (a fit). Only withhold support if you have both a fit for your partner's minor-suit opener and a biddable major-suit: it's wiser to play in the higher-scoring major.

• 'Jump' support (i.e. a bid from 1♥ to 3♥ or 1♥ to 4♥) shows you have four+ card support, but single raises of a major (i.e. from 1♥ to 2♥ or 1♠ to 2♠) may contain just three-card support.

(b) Bid 2♠. You have only five high-card points, but how valuable that singleton heart rates to be. Upgrade.

(c) Go straight to 4♠. Don't mention your diamonds as it will only confuse matters and block your four-card support for spades. You know that spades should be trumps so let your partner know.

Responding without a fit

Most of the time you will not be able to support the suit your partner opened. In these instances, you remain in the 'trying-to-find-a-fit' stage of the bidding, where your plan is to bid your longest suit at the lowest level.

Let's consider your response to a 1♣ opener with the following hands:

(a)	(b)	(c)
♠ J9742	♠ 972	♠ K943
♥ Q742	♥ KJ94	♥ 98
♦ K5	♦ A32	♦ A1032
♣ 85	♣ J96	♣ 952

(a) Bid 1♠ – your longest suit at the lowest level – and await developments. You have a minimum point count but must respond as your partner may have 19 points.

(b) Bid 1♥ (and not no-trumps), even though your hand is balanced. Whereas an opener's bidding strategy is dependent on the balanced/unbalanced issue, a responder's is not. Indeed a responder should only respond in no-trumps as a last resort, and should always prefer a suit that can be bid at the One level.

(c) Bid 1♦. Always respond the cheaper of two four-card suits.

Strategy for responding to a suit opener

- With a choice of four-card suits, respond with the suit that will allow the cheapest bid (i.e. the bid that comes first as you work up the bidding hierarchy on p. 22).
- With two five-card suits, it's more economical to bid the higher-ranking first, and plan to bid the lower-ranking one next (to remember this, think 'high-five').
- As responder, try to bid a suit to a suit. Only respond no-trumps to a suit opener as a last resort.

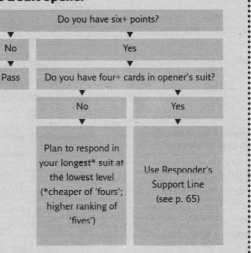

Do you have six+ points?	
No	Yes
Pass	Do you have four+ cards in opener's suit?
	No	Yes
	Plan to respond in your longest* suit at the lowest level (*cheaper of 'fours'; higher ranking of 'fives')	Use Responder's Support Line (see p. 65)

Let's look at three more examples. Your partner opens 1♥, what would you respond with the following hands?

(a)	(b)	(c)
♠ J942	♠ J2	♠ AJ10643
♥ 72	♥ 4	♥ 98
♦ KQ75	♦ KJ932	♦ 32
♣ AJ5	♣ AK986	♣ J92

(a) Respond 1♣ – the cheaper of the four-card suits in bidding terms.

(b) Respond 2♦ – it's best to bid the higher of two five-card suits first.

(c) Respond 1♠. But note that if your spades were clubs or diamonds, you should feel uneasy about bidding 2♣/♦ with such a weak hand.

The Rule of 14

If your hand suggests that you should respond in a new suit, there's a big difference (an extra trick!) between responding in a new suit at the One level and responding in a new suit at the Two level. The latter shouldn't be done lightly – and certainly not with only six or seven points and four weak cards (even though these would be perfectly admissible at the One level).

The Rule of 14 (when to bid a suit at the Two level)

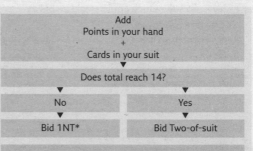

The Rule of 14 (see the diagram above) is a useful guideline, combining points in your hand with the number of cards in the suit you wish to bid, and telling you whether you should bid a new suit at the Two level. If the points in your hand added to the number of cards in your suit reach 14, you can bid Two-of-a-suit according to the Rule of 14; if the total is fewer then you must find an alternative bid.

The 'dustbin' 1NT

When you've failed the Rule of 14, and thus can't bid a new suit at the Two level, your last resort is to bid 1NT.

This is often termed the 'dustbin' 1NT because it's what you bid with hands that don't fit anywhere else.

Don't think of the 1NT response as a proper no-trump bid – it doesn't necessarily show a balanced hand (indeed responder could have a void and/or a seven-card suit). It's a stalling manoeuvre, in practice showing six, seven, eight or occasionally nine points (but never more). It shows you don't have four-card support for your partner, or a higher-ranking four-card suit (which could freely be bid at the One level with just six points).

Let's consider the best response to a 1♥ opener with the following hands:

(a)	(b)	(c)	(d)
♠ 842	♠ 962	♠ 1043	♠ 10643
♥ 6	♥ 102	♥ -	♥ J3
♦ KQ9752	♦ K102	♦ Q632	♦ AJ1052
♣ J53	♣ AQ1085	♣ AJ9852	♣ J4

(a) A classic 1NT response. Six diamonds and six points fails the Rule of 14. If opener rebids 2♣, you should respond 2♦. By going via the 'dustbin' 1NT to bid your diamonds you're showing a weak hand with long diamonds. Your partner will get the message and is likely to pass. Whereas if you immediately respond 2♦, your partner will be forced to bid again, and if his next bid is, say, 3♣, you are likely to score badly.

(b) Bid 2♣. You satisfy the Rule of 14.

(c) Bid 1NT. You fail the Rule of 14 – remember that 1NT is just a point-count bid, and doesn't show a balanced hand.

(d) Bid 1♠, which shows four+ spades and six+ points. At first glance this appears to be a 1NT response (it fails the Rule of 14), but don't be caught out: this ignores the four-card spade suit. Never respond 1NT when you can bid a suit at the One level.

Note that if your partner opened 1♠ (as opposed to 1♥), with hands (a), (c) and (d) – i.e. the hands that failed the Rule of 14 – you should raise to 2♠. A single-major raise (1♠-2♠) doesn't guarantee four-card support in the same way as a jump raise (1♠-3♠, 1♠-4♠).

After the 'dustbin' 1NT response

When opener hears a 1NT response from his partner, he knows he's facing a weak hand: just six, seven, eight or occasionally nine points. He also knows that responder doesn't have four-card support for his opening suit, or a higher-ranking four-card suit. The likelihood is that the partnership doesn't belong in game, so it's a question of finding a safe resting spot at the Two level. Opener can 'bid out a five-four shape' (i.e. introduce a four-card suit), though not if it's higher-ranking, because of responder's weak hand. Alternatively, he can repeat a six-card suit.

For example, after opening 1♥ and hearing a 1NT response, opener should:

(a)	(b)	(c)
♠ J2	♠ A62	♠ AJ43
♥ AQ642	♥ KJ9842	♥ Q9852
♦ KQ75	♦ K6	♦ K2
♣ J5	♣ 86	♣ A10

(a) Bid 2♦, showing the five-four shape.

(b) Rebid 2♥ with the six-card suit.

(c) Pass and hope that your partner can scrape together seven tricks. The alternative, a 2♠ bid (showing the five-four shape), would be unwise as the 1NT response has shown that your partner doesn't have four spades to make a fit.

Returning to responder, let's say the bidding has begun 1♥-1NT-2♦, as in (a) above. Bearing in mind opener has shown five hearts and four diamonds (minimum), responder is in a good position if she has three hearts (the partnership has a heart fit), or four diamonds (a diamond fit). She'll bid 2♥ with the former, and pass with the latter – leaving the partnership with a Two-level bid in each case.

For example, after the bidding sequence 1♥-1NT-2♦, responder should:

(a)	(b)	(c)
♠ J2	♠ J62	♠ 643
♥ 72	♥ J6	♥ 8
♦ J875	♦ 109	♦ Q32
♣ AJ542	♣ AJ9863	♣ KJ6432

(a) Pass.

(b) Bid 2♥. There's no fit, except perhaps clubs, but going up to the Three level to find out would be too risky; hearts is the best option as there are at least seven trumps.

(c) Pass. At least there will be seven trumps.

More on overcalling

An overcall, as you've already learnt, is a bid after the opponents have opened the bidding. It is completely different from an opening bid. Where opener and responder can look forward to a (potentially) lengthy communication of information leading to a choice of trump suit, an overcaller can expect much less time to convey her message. Therefore, any suit bid by an overcaller is a strong request for trumps. Overcall a four-card suit or even a weak five-card suit and you may become sandwiched between two strong hands, with unhappy results.

Suit Quality Overcall Test (SQOT)

The Suit Quality Overcall Test (SQOT – pronounced 'squat') is a test to see whether your preferred suit – which must be at least five cards in length – is strong enough to overcall. Note that this test is meant to be a helpful guideline, not a hard and fast rule.

must know
• Normally overcall at the lowest level – at the One level if possible.
• As a guide: around six high-card points is a minimum for a One-level overcall, and eight for a Two-level overcall.

The SQOT is as follows:
- Add the number of cards in your suit (which must be five+) to the number of 'honour' cards in the suit (honour cards are the top five cards in a suit: A, K, Q, J and 10).
- Only overcall (at the lowest level) if the total reaches the number of tricks you have to make in your bid.

For example, with a suit of KQ842, you have five cards and two honours (counting one for the king and one for the queen), giving a SQOT of seven. You can bid for a contract of up to seven tricks. Or with a suit of AQ1062, five cards and three honours (counting one each for the ace, queen and ten), you have a SQOT of eight so can bid for a contract of up to eight tricks (level One or Two).

Let's consider whether you should overcall with the following hands after a 1♣ opener from your right-hand opponent:

(a)	(b)	(c)	(d)
♠ KQ1094	♠ Q74	♠ J7632	♠ AKJ6
♥ 63	♥ K98742	♥ Q3	♥ 65
♦ 75	♦ K8	♦ AQ4	♦ K1086
♣ Q842	♣ 62	♣ QJ7	♣ 1074

(a) Definitely overcall 1♠. With a suit of five cards and three honours (remember that ten is an honour), your spade suit has a SQOT of eight, ample for bidding a seven-trick contract. In spite of your meagre point count, a bid such as this is winning bridge for the following reasons:
(i) It may lead to making a spade contract. As the highest-ranked suit, spades often wins the bidding.
(ii) It may lead to a 'sacrifice bid', which means outbidding your opponents even though you expect to lose, because the points

'above the line' (see scoring on pp. 220–1) that you concede will be less valuable to the opponents than the points below the line you give away for them making their bid.

(iii) It may mess up your opponents' bidding, e.g. your 1♠ bid prevents your left-hand opponent from responding 1♥; bidding 2♥ requires a much stronger hand, so he'll either pass, perhaps missing a heart fit, or chance a 2♥ bid and perhaps get too high.

(iv) Even if you lose the bidding, at least you've told your partner which suit to lead.

(b) Overcall 1♥. Your suit is less strong than (a), but you have a sixth card to compensate.

(c) Pass. Your point count is reasonable, but your trick-taking power is poor. Defence is probably best on this deal.

(d) Pass. You should never overcall on a four-card suit, however strong.

Now consider which of the following hands you as Overcaller No. 2 should bid (see diagram on p. 74). The auction has proceeded 1♣-1♠-2♦ (your left-hand opponent opened 1♣; partner overcalled 1♠; right-hand opponent responded 2♦).

(e)	(f)	(g)
♠ 52	♠ 2	♠ Q108
♥ KQ9642	♥ A9852	♥ AQ1032
♦ K5	♦ Q1074	♦ 62
♣ 865	♣ QJ3	♣ 952

(e) A perfect 2♥ bid. This shows, most importantly, a suit you'd like to mention to your partner (satisfying SQOT), and, secondarily, an acceptable point count for the Two-level bid.

(f) You should keep quiet – your hearts are well short of the required suit quality for a Two-level overcall. You have a useful defensive hand on a deal where it's quite likely that neither side has a fit (a 'misfit').

(g) You have a heart suit that satisfies 'SQOT'. But a principle that exists throughout bidding is 'fit first'; particularly if it's a major suit, telling your partner of a known eight-card fit is a top priority. Bid 2♠ – a known fit because your partner has guaranteed at least five spades for his overcall. Indeed if you do not support spades now, partner will never believe that you have three of them.

Strategies around the table

Here are the basic strategies of the four players around the table.
Note that 'Overcaller No. 2' uses the same strategy as 'Overcaller No. 1'.

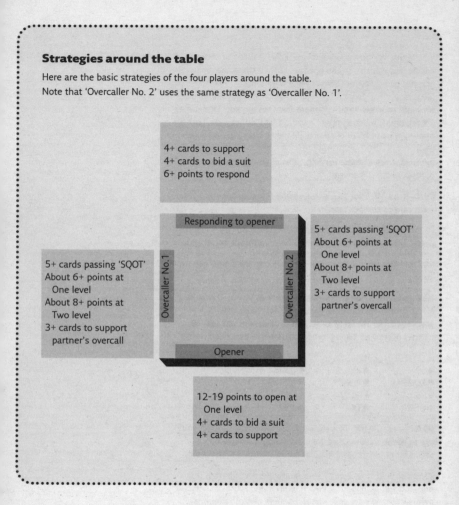

4+ cards to support
4+ cards to bid a suit
6+ points to respond

Responding to opener

5+ cards passing 'SQOT'
About 6+ points at
  One level
About 8+ points at
  Two level
3+ cards to support
  partner's overcall

Overcaller No.1

Overcaller No. 2

5+ cards passing 'SQOT'
About 6+ points at
  One level
About 8+ points at
  Two level
3+ cards to support
  partner's overcall

Opener

12-19 points to open at
  One level
4+ cards to bid a suit
4+ cards to support

Supporting an overcall

By overcalling, your partner shows five (+) cards in a
suit. You as second overcaller need three cards to
support his overcall to achieve a fit. However the
more cards you hold, the bolder you can be. You
should try and push the bidding as high as possible
depending on the degree of fit:

Bidding to the 'level of the fit' has proved amazingly effective in damage limitation. For you'll generally concede less than if you let your opponents reach their optimum contract. Plus you might make the contract.

The same principle applies both when the second overcaller supports the first overcall, and in the bidding that follows. In the subsequent bidding, the original overcaller should raise the bidding a further level if he has an extra trump card above those already shown. In this way the overcalling partnership always bids for the number of tricks equal to their number of trumps, i.e. bids to the level of the fit.

Let's consider what you (as second overcaller) should bid with the following hands, after 1♣-1♠-2♦ (your left-hand opponent opened 1♣; partner overcalled 1♠; right-hand opponent responded 2♦):

(a)	(b)	(c)
♠ J92	♠ QJ62	♠ K9742
♥ A9642	♥ 42	♥ J10732
♦ 75	♦ 74	♦ 2
♣ 762	♣ J8632	♣ 82

(a) 2♠. You know of the eight-card spade fit (your partner must have five+ spades in order to over-call, and you have three), so you should bid for eight tricks.

(b) 3♠. There are nine+ spades (your partner's five+ and your four), so bid for nine tricks.

(c) 4♠. There's a known ten-card fit, so bid for ten tricks. Bidding 2♠, then 3♠, then 4♠ is far less effective than immediately jumping to 4♠. The jump bid gives your opponents less time to exchange information about each other's hands.

Useful tip

There are times when you may want to bid above or below the 'level of the fit'. For example, if you have a poor distribution and a very low point count, you may be well advised to bid one fewer than the level of the fit.

Overcalling no-trumps

You need a stronger hand to overcall 1NT than to open 1NT. Specifically, you need more points and a 'stopper' in the suit(s) bid by your opponents.

A stopper, as the name suggests, is a series of cards held by you that will stop the opponent from running away with tricks in their suit. Aces and kings make the best stoppers, but queens and jacks may

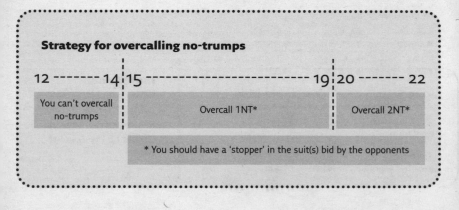

Strategy for overcalling no-trumps

12 ------- 14	15 ------------------------- 19	20 ------- 22
You can't overcall no-trumps	Overcall 1NT*	Overcall 2NT*
	* You should have a 'stopper' in the suit(s) bid by the opponents	

also act as 'stops' if other reasonable cards are held. A4, K5, QJ3, J1096 are all examples of stoppers; Q3, 186, 8742 are not strong enough to be stoppers.

You also need a good point count. For example, if you have a balanced hand with 12, 13 or 14 points and are ready to open 1NT, but your right-hand opponent opens the bidding in front of you with 1♥, then you should not overcall 1NT. Knowing that your opponent has at least 12 points should be a warning that you may be sandwiched between two strong hands.

Let's consider what you should bid if your right-hand opponent opens 1♦ and you have the following hands:

(a)	(b)	(c)
♠ AJ92	♠ AQ72	♠ KJ2
♥ 42	♥ AK2	♥ AQ
♦ AQ5	♦ AQ94	♦ 8762
♣ KQ98	♣ J10	♣ KQ62

(a) You have a perfect 1NT overcall: 15–19 points and a good stopper in the opposing diamonds. Note that you don't need stoppers in all the suits, so the heart weakness is acceptable.

(b) Overcall 2NT. You have the same strength of hand as a 2NT opener plus a diamond stopper.

(c) Pass. You have enough points to overcall 1NT, but no diamond stopper.

must know

A 1NT overcall shows a stronger hand than a 1NT opener: where a 1NT opener shows a balanced hand with 12, 13 or 14 points, a 1NT overcall typically shows 15–19 points and a 'stopper' in the suit(s) bid by the opponents.

Useful tip

Pass is often the best bid in bridge, especially if your hand doesn't meet the requirements for opening or overcalling.

Fulfilling your contract

Bidding and play, though separate phases of the game, are inextricably linked. At an integral level, how you make your tricks as declarer depends on whether your contract is in trumps or not.

must know

Besides top tricks, you're likely to need extra tricks to fulfil your contract. There are three ways to make extra tricks that don't require a trump suit: by Force, Length and Position (to remember, think 'FLaP').

Tricks without using trumps

When dummy is tabled, you as declarer should be in the habit (particularly in no-trumps) of counting the 'top tricks'. You can then see how many extra tricks you need in order to fulfil your contract. Top tricks are those you can make before losing the lead in that suit.

Let's first look at trick-taking with trumps taken out of the equation.

Cashing tricks in the right order

When cashing top tricks, you've already seen that the order of playing the sequential top cards can be important (the Unblocking Rule on p. 15).

Have a look at the following examples. How many top tricks do the suit holdings contain, and in which order would you (as declarer) play them?

(a)	(b)	(c)
Dummy	Dummy	Dummy
AQ4	AQ4	Q2
Declarer	Declarer	Declarer
KJ3	KJ32	AKJ43

(a) Three top tricks. With equal length holdings and only three cards in each, it's unavoidable that two of your top cards will cash together in the same trick (making one worthless). Here it doesn't matter which order the top cards are played.

(b) Adding the two to your holding gives a fourth trick – provided you use one top card per trick. Order does matter here. Lead ace first, then queen, then low to king-jack.

(c) Four top tricks. Start with queen, lead to ace-king-jack, then (subject to the opposing split) your fifth card is likely to be a length winner.

The first two ways of making extra tricks without using a trump suit (by force and by length) were outlined in chapter 2. We'll now look at these in detail, together with a third way (by position).

By force

This method of making extra tricks involves flushing out opposing higher card(s) and promoting your lower cards.

must know
Force winners don't depend on how many cards each opponent holds, nor on which opponent holds the missing high card(s). Provided you can afford to lose the lead, this method is risk-free.

Let's consider how many tricks can be made using the force method with the following suit holdings, split between the two hands, dummy and declarer:

(a)	(b)	(c)
K7	QJ109	J975
QJ104	64	1086

(a) Three tricks. Play king first to remove ace (the Unblocking Rule applies). You lose that trick, but win the next three. Note that if the opponents choose not to win ('duck') their ace, your king is promoted into an extra force winner. You can then lead to queen-jack-ten to force it out.

(b) Ace and king can be forced out (note that Q, J, 10 and 9 are of equal value here) to establish two force winners.

(c) One trick, after ace, king and queen have been flushed out.

By length

This method of making extra tricks involves exhausting the opponents of all their cards in a suit in which you have longer length.

Now consider how many tricks can be made with the following suit holdings:

(a)	(b)	(c)
AQ42	AQ642	A7642
K53	K53	K53

(a) Cashing the three top cards (king first) will make the fourth card (in the top holding) a length winner if the suit is split three-three between the opposition. (Unfortunately, four-two is more likely.)

(b) Cashing the three top cards (king first) will make two length winners (in the top hand) provided the suit splits three-two (it usually will). If the split is four-one, you can lose the fourth round and, provided you can return to the top hand, enjoy a fifth-round length winner instead.

(c) Cash the king-ace and, assuming both opponents have followed (revealing their expected three-two split), lose the third round to gain two length winners in the top hand. Note: given that you have to lose a trick in order to make the two long cards, you should probably give up the first round. On regaining the lead, you can cash the king, then the ace, and be in the right hand to enjoy the two long cards (assuming a three-two split).

By position (the 'finesse')

The third method of making extra tricks, 'by position' (also known as the 'finesse') involves promoting a card in a suit when the opponents have a higher card in the same suit. Here is the most basic situation, beginning with the declarer and dummy's suit holding:

K2
facing
43

You'd like to promote the king, even though the opponents hold the ace. There is no point leading the king: whichever opponent holds the ace will simply beat it with their ace. Equally, there's no point leading the low card accompanying the king (the two): the opponents will win the trick with a middling card, saving the ace for the king. The only possible way to win the trick is if:

- you lead from the opposite hand to the card you're trying to promote (in this case, the king), and
- the second player holds the higher card (here, the ace) rather than the fourth player.

Assuming both opponents are equally likely to hold the ace, the chances of your king being promoted into a trick are exactly 50-50.

Let's look at a few examples – the declarer and dummy suit holdings are shown in each case:

(a)	(b)	(c)	(d)
AQ	AQJ	A42	J2
53	753	Q53	AK43

In (a) you're trying to promote the queen, so must lead from the opposite hand. Lead the three and, assuming the second player plays low, play the queen. If the second player holds the king, your queen is promoted: your finesse has succeeded. If the fourth player holds the king, he'll beat the queen with his king and your finesse has failed.

In (b) you're trying to promote the queen and jack. Lead the three to the jack. If this loses to the king, at least you've promoted your queen. However if your jack wins (you now assume the second player holds the king), go back to the bottom hand (in another suit) and repeat the finesse, leading to the queen.

In (c) you're trying to promote the queen, so lead from the opposite hand. You can cash the ace first, but the key play is to lead the two to the queen. If the second player holds the king, then he can't prevent your queen from being promoted. Of course, he can play high with the king and win the trick, but your queen will then be a master. If he plays low, you will still score an extra trick with your queen. But if the king is sitting 'over the queen' (fourth-player position), then the queen will lose to the king, and your finesse will have failed.

In (d) you're trying to promote your jack. Lead the three, and hope that the second player holds the queen. If he does, whether he plays it or not, your jack will be promoted into a positional winner.

Useful tip

On many deals you should delay taking a finesse because of the risk of it not going your way. However, sometimes you'll need to finesse early in a deal to reap its benefits, for example, when a finesse opportunity occurs within a long suit that you're trying to establish, or within the trump suit.

Making extra tricks without using trumps

Here is a summary of how to make extra tricks without using trumps.

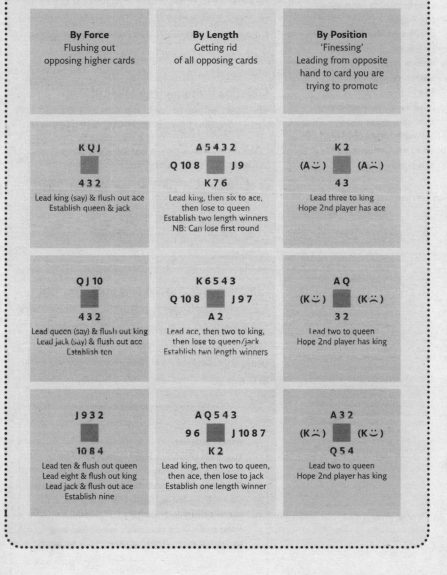

By Force	By Length	By Position
Flushing out opposing higher cards	Getting rid of all opposing cards	'Finessing' Leading from opposite hand to card you are trying to promote
K Q J 4 3 2 Lead king (say) & flush out ace Establish queen & jack	A 5 4 3 2 Q 10 8 ☐ J 9 K 7 6 Lead king, then six to ace, then lose to queen Establish two length winners NB: Can lose first round	K 2 (A ☺) ☐ (A ☹) 4 3 Lead three to king Hope 2nd player has ace
Q J 10 4 3 2 Lead queen (say) & flush out king Lead jack (say) & flush out ace Establish ten	K 6 5 4 3 Q 10 8 ☐ J 9 7 A 2 Lead ace, then two to king, then lose to queen/jack Establish two length winners	A Q (K ☺) ☐ (K ☹) 3 2 Lead two to queen Hope 2nd player has king
J 9 3 2 10 8 4 Lead ten & flush out queen Lead eight & flush out king Lead jack & flush out ace Establish nine	A Q 5 4 3 9 6 ☐ J 10 8 7 K 2 Lead king, then two to queen, then ace, then lose to jack Establish one length winner	A 3 2 (K ☹) ☐ (K ☺) Q 5 4 Lead two to queen Hope 2nd player has king

Tricks with trumps

You've learnt that finding a trump suit is the primary task of the bidding, and that eight cards constitute a fit. Now we'll consider how to make best use of the trump suit once it's chosen. The first important task is counting missing trump cards so you know when the opposition have run out of their supply.

Counting trumps and the Rule of One

The best method of counting trumps is to focus only on the missing cards:

- Work out how many trumps are missing.
- Think in terms of their likely split.
- Each time an opponent plays a trump, reduce the number of missing cards by one.
- When you reach zero, trumps have been 'drawn'.

Avoid the method of counting trumps in tricks (i.e. one round draws four trumps, including yours; two rounds draws eight; etc, up to 13 trumps). You'll miscount the outstanding missing trumps using this method if you forget you trumped early in the deal.

Let's consider how to keep track of missing trumps with the
following holdings:

(a)			(b)	
Dummy			Dummy	
AK2			A32	
West	East	West		East
Declarer			Declarer	
Q6543			K87654	

In (a) there are five missing trumps. The most probable split of
this odd number of missing cards between the opposition is
as even as possible: 3-2. Cash the ace-king (high cards from
the shorter length first) and, if both opponents follow twice
(thereby confirming the 3-2 split), you know there's just one
trump missing. Because the last trump is smaller than your
queen, and not destined to make a trick, lead to your queen.
Trumps are drawn.

In (b) there are four missing trumps. The split of this even
number of missing cards between the opposition is more likely
to be 3-1 than 2-2. Cash the ace, and if both opponents follow
you know that two missing trumps remain. These you hope will
fall when you now lead to your king. If one opponent follows
and the other throws away another suit, this confirms the split
3-1 and one trump outstanding. The trump outstanding is
higher than yours. It doesn't make sense to waste more trumps
removing a trump that will win a trick anyway (the Rule of One)
so abandon trumps now, leaving the last trump at large, and
concentrate on other suits.

Now we'll see how the finesse, introduced on
p.80, can be used to draw opposing trumps.

Dummy
432

Declarer
AQJ65

Aim to promote the queen-jack via finesses, so you need to start from the opposite hand (by winning the previous trick in dummy so you can lead from dummy's hand). Lead the two from dummy and, assuming the second player plays low, finesse your jack. This wins if the last player (the second defender) follows suit with a low card. Following this round you can count missing trumps down from five to three.

Now, assuming you can return to dummy in another suit, lead the three to queen. If the last player plays low a second time, you succeed in finessing your queen. You now know there's just one trump outstanding (the king). Cash the ace, felling the king, and you have drawn trumps without loss. You have taken full advantage of the favourable layout: the king sitting 'under' the ace-queen-jack, and the suit splitting three-two.

When to draw trumps

The advantage of drawing trumps early is that you get rid of two of the opposing trumps on each trick, then can play out your winners with no danger of them being trumped. The disadvantage is that you also get rid of two of your trumps per trick, trumps that may have scored separately (making two tricks).

The question of when to draw trumps boils down to one main issue: can you (as declarer) use the trumps in the hand with the shorter trump length (usually dummy's) that will fall helplessly under yours if you draw trumps early. In other words, if there's a way to score tricks with dummy's trumps then it's worth delaying the drawing of trumps from the opposition. This can occur if you have a short side suit (a non-trump suit) in dummy that can be

oided (played out until no cards are left): this then
enables your extra card(s) in that suit to be trumped
before dummy's trumps have been drawn.

Here's the routine for deciding whether to delay
drawing trumps so you can trump in dummy:

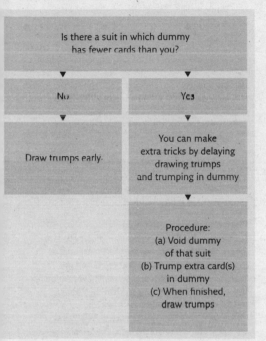

Is there a suit in which dummy
has fewer cards than you?

No → Draw trumps early.

Yes → You can make
extra tricks by delaying
drawing trumps
and trumping in dummy

Procedure:
(a) Void dummy
of that suit
(b) Trump extra card(s)
in dummy
(c) When finished,
draw trumps

Useful tip

When defending, and you see declarer trying to void
dummy of a suit preparatory to trumping in dummy,
the best strategy is to lead trumps. You may be able to
remove all of dummy's trumps before they can be
used for trumping.

Let's consider when you (as declarer) should draw trumps. On the following deals you have a game contract of 4♠ to fulfil, on ♦Q lead:

(a)	(b)
Dummy (N)	Dummy (N)
♠ Q32	♠ Q32
♥ 32	♥ 32
♦ K432	♦ K432
♣ J432	♣ J432
Declarer (S)	Declarer (S)
♠ AKJ54	♠ AKJ54
♥ AK4	♥ 654
♦ A65	♦ A65
♣ 76	♣ AK

Bidding (applies to both deals)

S	N
1 ♠	2 ♠ (i)
4 ♠ (ii)	End

First, a note about the bidding:
(i) Your partner (N) makes a single major raise (to 2♠), which doesn't guarantee four-card support (unlike the jump raises 1♠-3♠/4♠). Given her high honour in trumps, and the ability to trump, this is a more sensible option than the nebulous 1NT response she could have made.
(ii) Facing 6–9 points, you (as South) now know the values for game are present and can bid the contract 4♠.

Trick-taking:
On both layouts, you have (assuming trumps don't split five-nil) nine top tricks (five trumps and two ace-kings). This is one short of the ten you need for game. On each layout dummy has fewer hearts than you, and therein lies the key to the tenth trick.

(a) You can win the diamond lead with ♦A, then cash ♥AK, thus voiding dummy of hearts. Next lead ♥4, and trump it (with ♠2). Assuming this is not overtrumped (unlikely – it would mean West has six hearts), ♠2 turns into a trick (an extra trick). The work done, you can now play ♠Q, ♠3 to ♠AKJ (drawing trumps), and nine top tricks have become ten. Game made.

(b) You have more work voiding dummy of hearts this time, but it's still possible, and you'll generate an extra trick as a result. Win ♦A, then lead a heart. The defence wins this trick, and do their best to return a trump, trying to remove dummy's trumps. However, they fail as you can win ♠Q and lead a second heart, thus voiding dummy of hearts. The defence win this and lead a second trump. You win ♣J and now lead a third heart and trump it with dummy's last trump. This is the extra trick. Cross to ♣K, draw trumps, and claim ten tricks, as opposed to the nine you started with.

must know
While trumping in dummy (as the short trump hand) is a good idea, trumping in your hand (as the long trump hand) is normally not. This is because you rate to make tricks with the trumps in your hand anyway, by virtue of their length and strength.

More on defence

Many people regard defence as the most difficult part of the game. I'm not convinced this should be the case as defence is two heads versus the declarer's one (dummy isn't involved). Provided the two partners help one another in their shared goal, defending becomes an effective – and rewarding – experience.

Opening lead

Over half of all contracts that start life in the balance are decided by the choice of opening lead – the first and only card the defence play without sight of dummy. The strategies introduced in chapter 2 will now be elaborated here.

Defending against no-trumps

Selecting the best card to lead is a two-stage process: picking the suit, and choosing the card within the suit.

Picking the suit

As we saw in chapter 2, your basic plan as defender is to lead a long suit. This should be your longest suit unless (a) your partner has bid (in which case choose her suit), or (b) the opponents have already bid the suit (in which case choose your second longest). Both you and your partner should play the chosen suit whenever you are on lead – to exhaust the declarer and dummy of their cards in the suit. You can then go on to cash defensive length winners.

Picking the card

The standard card to lead is the fourth from the top.

Let's consider what you should lead against the auction 1NT-3NT with each of the following hands:

(a)
♠ KJ942
♥ 8
♦ K105
♣ J985

(b)
♠ J9762
♥ KJ952
♦ 32
♣ 3

(c)
♠ KQJ72
♥ 986
♦ 9832
♣ 9

(a) Lead ♠4 (fourth highest of the longest suit).

(b) Lead ♥5 (fourth highest of the longest and strongest suit). If your partner has ♥A, you may be able to run the first five tricks (in hearts), defeating 3NT before declarer has even started. Whereas ♠A in your partner's hand wouldn't be enough to take five spade tricks (on a spade lead). Relying on your partner for the minimum required to defeat the contract is a sound principle throughout the defence.

(c) In this case if you lead ♠7 (fourth highest), Declarer may win a cheap trick with ♠10. Instead you should force out ♠A, thus promoting your high honours with low cards once everybody has run out of the suit (which is quite likely). Follow this 'rule': when you have three touching high cards in your long suit (AKQ, KQJ, QJ10, J109 and 1098), lead the top of the run rather than the fourth from the top: ♠K in this instance.

must know

An exception to the rule of leading the fourth highest of the longest and strongest suit against a no-trump contract is when you have three touching high cards in your long suit (AKQ, KQJ, QJ10, J109 and 1098). In this instance lead the top card of the run rather than the fourth highest – see example (c) left.

Defending against trumps

Selecting what to lead against trumps is, again, a two-stage process:

Picking the suit

This is not simply a matter of leading from your best suit. Good holdings, particularly those that include the ace without the king, are best left intact. Sometimes there's a clear choice of lead, but in other cases the best approach is to eliminate the bad opening leads and see what's left. The alternatives can be divided as follows:

Opening leads against trump contracts

Good lead	Average lead	Poor lead
ace-king (the best)	doubleton	ace without king (the worst)
singleton (not trumps)	trumps	
other high-card sequences of two	suits headed by broken honours (e.g. AQ, KJ, AJ, Q10, etc)	
partner's suit	suits with only small cards ('rubbish')	
	opposing suits	

Note that these are guidelines, not rules. For example, a singleton lead may work: your partner may win the ace, and lead a second round for you to trump; or it may not: the declarer may win and promptly draw all your trumps. However, there are undisputed best and worst leads:

• The best lead: ace from ace-king
Leading an ace when you hold both the ace and the king gives you a free look at dummy (as you still have the boss card of the suit). You can then choose whether to continue the suit (by playing the king), or switch to another suit (you should have a good idea which one based on what you see in dummy).

• The worst lead: leading away from an ace
This shows why not to lead away from an ace:

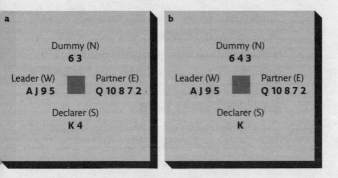

In (a), left to his own devices, declarer will try to promote his king via a finesse. He'll lead from dummy towards his king, and hope that the player on his right (East) holds the ace. In this case West holds the ace so the king will lose to the ace. However, declarer will succeed in scoring a trick with his king if West leads the suit: leading the ace promotes declarer's king; leading low allows declarer to use the king to take East's queen.

In (b) we see again the perils of leading away from an ace: declarer scores his singleton king, and can then trump the ace.

Picking the card

The leading card within the chosen suit should be one that:

(i) maximizes the trick-taking potential for the defence.

(ii) conveys a message to your partner about your holding, e.g. whether you like it/hate it and which high cards you have. The diagram on p. 94 shows how the two defenders can impart information to one another by virtue of the card they pick to lead.

(iii) is the top card if you're leading from just two

must know

• Ace from ace-king is the best lead against a trump contract.
• Don't lead away from an ace at Trick one to a trump contract. Note that it's acceptable to lead away from an ace at Trick one to a no-trump contract (a cheap trick is okay if there's length to be made), or after dummy has been tabled, both in no-trumps and trumps.

cards (a doubleton) – think 'top from two'. This way, when you next follow lower, your partner can suspect that you've run out of the suit (although admittedly it's also possible that you started with a 'high-for-hate' lead if you lead with a nine, eight, seven or six – see the 'lead line' diagram below).

(iv) is the normal card if you're leading your partner's suit (which, incidentally, is a good thing to do), i.e. don't automatically lead top of your partner's suit (commonplace some years ago); lead instead the card that you'd lead if your partner hadn't bid the suit, e.g. the highlighted card from: K6**2**, **8**4, 9**8**2, **J**102, **Q**4.

The lead line

	Honour leads	High spot cards	Low spot cards
The card	ace king queen jack ten	nine eight seven six	five four three two
What you show	king queen jack ten nine	Lead High for Hate, Lead Low for Like	

Honours: First, consider the lead of an honour (ace, king, queen, jack or ten). Such a lead shows that you hold the card immediately below, and denies the card immediately above (though it does not deny cards more than one above). Why lead top of a sequence (rather than, say, bottom)? Imagine holding the ace and your partner leads from king-queen. If he leads the king, you know not to play the ace; not so if he leads the queen.

Small cards: Now consider the lead of a 'spot' card (a ten or lower). This also carries a message: if you lead high (e.g. an eight) then you show lack of interest in the suit ('lead high for hate'); you probably don't want the lead returned. If you lead low (e.g. a three) then your partner's interpretation will be positive ('lead low for like').

Note that there is a 'grey area' around the five and six, which might be low or high.

Let's consider which card to select assuming you've decided to lead from the following holdings:

(a)	(b)	(c)	(d)	(e)	(f)
J1072	Q1095	9842	KJ63	74	AJ62

(a) Jack. This honour lead shows the ten and denies the queen.

(b) Ten. This shows the nine and denies the jack (but does not deny honours higher than this – as you can see).

(c) Eight or nine. (Lead 'high for hate'.) In effect, you're saying, 'Partner, I'm leading this suit in the hope that you have something useful. But please don't lead it back to me'.

(d) Three. (Lead 'low for like'.) This is a dangerous lead, but it will work well when your partner has either the ace or queen.

(e) Seven. ('Top from two'.)

(f) You shouldn't lead this suit at Trick one (don't lead 'away from an ace').

Now consider the 13 cards in your hand and decide which suit, and which card within the suit, you should use to lead. The opponents have bid 1♥-4♥.

(a)	(b)	(c)
♠ KJ6	♠ AQ54	♠ K108
♥ Q42	♥ 72	♥ 974
♦ 72	♦ J86	♦ Q86
♣ A9763	♣ QJ43	♣ A842

(a) No immediately obvious leads here, so first reject the bad ones. Away go clubs – leading away from an ace. Trumps are often a safe, give-away-nothing lead, but not when you hold the queen. Leading away from K-J is terribly risky – fine if your partner holds the queen or ace, but disastrous otherwise. The most prudent suit to lead – by a process of elimination if nothing else – is diamonds. Choose ♦7 ('top from two').

(b) ♣Q makes a good top-of-a-sequence lead.

(c) ♥4. The other suits would involve leading away from broken (i.e. non-sequential) honours, so it's safer to settle for a trump lead. Note that when leading a trump, you always lead low.

Defence issues

Now we'll turn to a few other matters of defence, including interpreting the lead and how to act on it. Remember 'TOP' (p. 43) – to focus on your Trick Target, Observe dummy and (perhaps most importantly) think about your Partner: she's on your side and you need to work out what she's doing.

Interpreting your partner's lead

As you've just learnt, if your partner leads:
• an honour, she's implying she holds the card immediately below, but not the card immediately above.
• a high spot card (e.g. a nine, eight or seven), she's leading 'high for hate', and you probably shouldn't return the suit.
• a low spot card (e.g. a two, three or four). She's leading 'low for like', and you probably should return the suit.

Switching

As defenders you hope to attack the declarer's weakest suit, but because the opening leader can't see dummy, you'll frequently begin on the wrong footing and need to 'switch' suits (this is where the tip 'Observe dummy' comes into play). In a trump contract, the dream holding to see in dummy is three small cards: being dummy's weakest suit, you should switch to it.

A typical trick

Each trick inherently consists of the first card ('the lead'), the second card, the third card and the last card. All have different roles. We've already looked at playing first (leading). Playing fourth (last) doesn't require much wisdom – aim to win the trick as cheaply as possible, otherwise follow with your lowest card.

There's a huge difference between a defender playing second and a defender playing third. Playing second, your partner has yet to play a card to the trick (he is last). The pressure is off: if you play low, the declarer–dummy playing third can't win a cheap trick because your partner will almost certainly beat the low-value card. Playing third, however, the pressure is high: if your partner has led low, and dummy, playing second, also plays low, if you play low yourself then declarer will win a cheap trick, so you must play a high card. Then if declarer wants to win the trick, he has to play an even higher card – if he doesn't have one, then you, as third player, win the trick.

Two important defensive guidelines emerge from this:

- Second player plays low.
- Third player plays high.

Second player plays low

If declarer leads a low card from his hand or dummy's, you should follow low. For example:

	North (Dummy)	
	K93	
West		East (you)
Q754		J82
	South (Declarer)	
	A106	

must know

In defence it is vital to know the number of tricks you need in order to defeat the declarer's contract. For example, if the contract is 4♥, then declarer must win ten tricks or more, and you need to win four tricks or more to defeat him. It is sometimes helpful to think of this as the defenders' contract.

must know
A defender playing
second to a trick should
normally play low on a
low card, but cover an
honour with an honour.

If declarer leads the three from dummy, you (East)
must not play the jack. If you do, declarer will win
with the ace and lead low to dummy's nine, thus
scoring all three tricks in the suit. You should follow
instead with the two (the eight is pointless, but
would survive here), then declarer wins no more
than his ace and king. Bear in mind that because
you are playing second to the trick, your partner
hasn't yet contributed a card. Declarer wins the
trick only if he plays a card higher than West's
highest card.

If declarer leads an honour from his hand or
dummy's, in most cases you should cover it (play a
high card), hence the catchphrase: 'Cover an honour
with an honour'. Covering an honour with an honour
won't always be the right thing to do, but it generally
works if you think you can promote a lower card
(such as a ten) for you or your partner. For example:

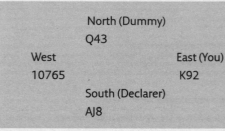

```
                    North (Dummy)
                    Q43
          West                        East (You)
          10765                       K92
                    South (Declarer)
                    AJ8
```

If dummy's queen is led, you must cover with the
king, sacrificing it to draw two of the opponents'
honours for one of yours (a good trade). In this way
declarer wins the ace and jack, but never scores the
dummy's queen.

Third player plays high
Let's look at an example to illustrate this guideline:

```
                    Dummy
                    642
    Partner                     You
    leads 3                     K105
                    Declarer
                    ?
```

Assume this is Trick one to a trump contract, but note that the principles apply to all tricks, including no-trumps. If your partner leads low, and dummy follows low, what should you do? Though you know declarer holds the ace (as your partner wouldn't underlead an ace at Trick one to a trump contract), you must play your king. It's imperative you force out declarer's ace, and stop him winning the trick with a lower card that's not meant to score.

The layout may easily be:

```
                    Dummy
                    642
    Partner                     You
    Q973                        K105
                    Declarer
                    AJ8
```

If you play the king, all declarer can score is the ace (your partner can later beat declarer's jack with the queen); but if you play the ten, declarer will score the jack and, later, the ace.

must know

If you are playing in third position on a trick, your partner has already played. If your partner's card can't win the trick, it's up to you to play high. You will prevent declarer from winning a cheap trick. Either your card will win the trick, or force a higher card from declarer.

Here's another example, this time in no-trumps:

```
                    Dummy
                    642
    Partner                     You
    leads 3                     KQ5
                    Declarer
                    ?
```

must know

Two points to remember as third player:

• Play high, but the cheaper of touching cards.

• In general, retain a high card to beat an unplayed picture card in dummy.

Clearly you must play the king or queen. Even though they are both equals, it matters to your partner which one you play and in this case you must play the cheaper of your highest cards. There's sound logic for reversing the usual rule for leads from touching high cards, as this example shows: say your partner leads from an ace (admissible in no-trumps and after Trick one in a trump contract), and your queen wins the trick, your partner now knows you have the king, otherwise declarer could have won the trick with it. However, if you played the king, your partner couldn't draw the same inference. (Indeed, given that you, as third player, should always play the cheaper of touching high cards, playing the king in this case actually denies the queen.)

So when dummy has only low cards, the third player should always play high (but the cheaper of touching highest). However things change when dummy has an unplayed picture card, as in the next example:

```
              Dummy
              Q42 (plays the 2)
Partner                    You
leads 3                    K105
              Declarer
              ?
```

If this is Trick one to a trump contract, declarer is known to have the ace. There's no point in playing your king because declarer will take it with the ace, thereby promoting the dummy's queen. Play your ten instead, in the hope that your partner holds the jack. In this case, your ten will force out declarer's ace, thereby promoting your king. And even if you weren't sure who held the ace, playing the ten and retaining the king over dummy's queen would be a better strategy than playing the king.

Signalling

This refers to a legitimate form of defensive signalling in bridge (not the nudging and winking variety!). We've seen how you're able to send a message with your lead card (leading a high spot card for 'hate' and a low spot card for 'like'). You can also send a message when following suit to your partner's lead. Your priority is to play the proper card to maximize trick-taking (i.e. play high, but the cheaper of touching highest cards). For occasions when your card isn't able to contribute to the winning of the trick (e.g. your partner or dummy is winning the trick and you can't play higher), you can 'throw' a 'free card', which can be used to send messages.

The Attitude Signal:
● Throw low means: 'No, please don't continue the suit/I have nothing in this suit.'
● Throw high means: '(Aye) Yes please! Carry on – I have something for you here.'

For example:

```
                    Dummy
                    753
        West                East
        AKJ                 (i) 9642
                            (ii) Q962
                    Declarer
                    (i) Q108
                    (ii) 1084
```

West leads the ace, and must decide whether to continue the suit. Without a signal from his partner,

must know

The Attitude Signal – 'Throw high means aye, throw low means no' – applies on the first round of each suit, and also when you discard a card (see p. 103). It indicates whether you want your partner to continue in the current suit or switch to another suit.

it's a blind guess. If his partner holds the queen, it will be correct to continue – making three fast defensive tricks. But if declarer holds the queen, West will almost certainly be better off trying to 'find a way to his partner's hand' (in another suit – with dummy to guide him) aiming for a second round of this suit through declarer's queen, which would enable West to score his jack as well as his ace-king. With layout (i) West should switch suits; with layout (ii) he should carry on in the suit. Thanks to signalling, he knows what to do. In (i) East follows with the two ('throw low means no') – to warn off a continuation. In (ii) East follows with the nine – 'throw high means aye (yes, carry on)'; West now plays his king and jack.

In another example, a trump contract (with East holding trumps), West leads an ace. When should East signal with an encouraging high spot-card? The answer is East should assume that West holds ace-king and East should signal when she has third-round control of the suit – either (i) the queen, or (ii) a doubleton (enabling her to trump the third round). West will then lead out king and a third round. Note that West does not know if his partner is going to play the queen, or to trump it. Both outcomes, however, are desirable.

You can get by with no more than the Attitude Signal, but I should mention in passing two other signals – for different situations.

• The Count Signal: When declarer is leading a suit, it can be important to tell your defence partner how many cards you hold (she can then work out how many cards declarer holds): High means an Even number, Low means Odd ('HELO').

• The Suit-Preference Signal: When you're leading a suit for your partner to trump, a high spot card asks for the return of the higher-ranking other suit (not trumps); the return of a low spot card asks for the return of the lower-ranking suit.

Discarding

When you can't follow suit (and are not trumping) you discard, i.e. throw away a card. As we've just seen, the throwaway card can be used to send messages (the Attitude Signal: 'throw low means no, throw high means aye'). Use basic common sense when discarding: retain good cards, throw away bad ones – and don't forget to keep count. Other things to try to do when discarding are:

• Keep equal length with dummy (and declarer if you know how many cards he holds).
• Keep four-card suit lengths.

Useful tip

When discarding, be inclined to throw a worthless low spot card to say 'No' to a suit, rather than spare a potential trick-taking high spot card to say 'Yes'. If you eliminate one option, your partner will usually work out what to do.

want to know more?

• For more on doubles, see pp. 126–37.
• For more on slam bidding, see pp. 138–141.
• For bidding conventions, see pp. 142–5 and 158–169.
• For more on opening, responding and second bids, see pp. 170–189.
• For more on evaluating a bridge hand, see pp. 190–5.

Ten core deals

Example A

Dealer South

	North	
	♠ A74	
West	♥ K5	**East**
♠ 108632	♦ A8632	♠ 9
♥ A64	♣ J73	♥ 9872
♦ J		♦ Q1094
♣ A985		♣ K1042
	South	
	♠ KQJ5	
	♥ QJ103	
	♦ K75	
	♣ Q6	

The bidding:

South	West	North	East
1NT (i)	Pass	2NT (ii)	Pass
3NT (iii)	End		

(i) 12–14 points and a balanced hand.
(ii) Game invite, showing 11–12 balanced (-ish).
(iii) Accepting the invitation, as he holds a maximum.

The play:

West leads ♠3 – fourth from the top of his longest suit – and you as declarer first count your top tricks. You have four spades and two diamonds off the top (i.e. before you lose the lead). You need three extra tricks. The temptation is to look for them in the long diamonds. But, even if the opposing diamonds split 3-2, you will only be able to establish two extra tricks; plus diamonds might split four-one (as they in fact do). In fact three extra tricks are there for the taking by forcing out ♥A. Currently you have no top tricks in hearts, but, after forcing out ♥A, you will, regardless of who holds ♥A and irrespective of the heart split, promote three extra heart tricks.

Win ♠A and lead ♥K (high from the short side). Assuming West wins ♥A (if he doesn't win ['ducks'], then ♥K is an extra trick, and you can lead a second heart), you have promoted ♥QJ10. The defence can cash ♣AK when they win ♥A, but this will help *you*, promoting ♣J. More likely, they will press on with spades, enabling you to win, cash ♥QJ10, and follow with ♠AK and the remaining top spades. Nine tricks and game made.

If you remember just one thing about ...

Bidding: 2NT is the only game-invite facing a 1NT opener, and shows a balanced (-ish) 11–12 point hand.
Declaring: Look out for Force Winners – these do not depend on the opposing split, nor which opponent holds the high card(s) you are forcing out.
Defending: The normal no-trump lead is the fourth from the top of your longest suit.

Example B

Dealer South

```
                    North
                    ♠ AK
                    ♥ AQ975
      West          ♦ 75          East
      ♠ QJ854       ♣ J653        ♠ 1097
      ♥ 32                        ♥ J1086
      ♦ J9                        ♦ Q1086
      ♣ K1042       South         ♣ Q9
                    ♠ 632
                    ♥ K4
                    ♦ AK432
                    ♣ A87
```

The bidding:

South	West	North	East
1NT (i)	Pass (ii)	3♥ (iii)	Pass
3NT (iv)	End		

(i) 12–14 balanced. Note that a 5332 shape (even with a five-card major) is balanced.

(ii) Might consider a One-level overcall in spades (satisfying SQOT), but not a Two-level overcall.

(iii) The key bid. North's jump to 3♥ shows a game-forcing hand with precisely five hearts. Unusually, the 1NT opener is now required to bid again.

(iv) With three or more hearts, South would raise to 4♥. With a doubleton heart he must bid 3NT (there is no eight-card fit). Note that he cannot pass 3♥ – as it would not give game. (See figure on p. 63).

The play:

West leads ♠5 – fourth from the top of his longest suit – and, after surveying dummy, you count eight top tricks (two spades, three hearts, two diamonds and a club). Just one more needed, and you naturally look at the heart suit.

You have three top tricks, but two potential long cards in dummy, depending on the opposing split.

Winning ♠K, you cross to ♥K (high from the short) and return to ♥AQ. The hoped-for (but not expected – a missing even number of cards do not usually split evenly) three-three split does not materialize, West discarding (a diamond) on the third heart. Should you abandon hearts as a bad job?

Absolutely not! You must lose to win in bridge, and the key play is to give East his fourth-round heart winner. You can win any return from East (a spade is best, to set up West's remaining spades as defensive winners), and now dummy's fifth heart is a promoted length winner. Eight top tricks have become nine – which can now be played out. Game made.

If you remember just one thing about ...

Bidding: A jump to 3♥/♠ over 1NT shows a game-forcing hand with precisely five cards in the major.
Declaring: Don't be frightened to lose the lead, particularly early in the play. You have to 'lose to win' at bridge.
Defending: In no-trumps, it is normally best to return the suit partner led.

Example C

Dealer South

```
                        North
                        ♠ K63
                        ♥ 865
        West            ♦ Q754          East
        ♠ J9854         ♣ J64           ♠ 107
        ♥ Q107                          ♥ KJ43
        ♦ K103                          ♦ J82
        ♣ K8            South           ♣ AQ97
                        ♠ AQ2
                        ♥ A92
                        ♦ A96
                        ♣ 10532
```

The bidding:

South	West	North	East
1NT	Pass	Pass (i)	Pass

(i) Part-score zone, and, with no five-card suit in which to rescue, no reason to disturb partner.

The play:

West leads ♠5 – fourth from the top of the longest suit – and you count five top tricks. Needing two more, you should look for a combination of Position and Length in diamonds. First you must try to promote ♦Q via a finesse.

Win ♠5 in hand with (say) ♠Q, and lead ♦6 at Trick Two. By leading from the opposite hand to ♦Q, the card you are trying to promote, you will succeed in your finesse whenever West (the defender playing second) holds ♦K. Good news – West does hold ♦K. If he plays it, you play dummy's ♦4 and ♦Q will score later. Say West plays 'second hand low' (as he should), you play ♦Q and are pleased when it wins the trick. Five tricks have become six.

Now you look to set up a long diamond in dummy, possible if the suit splits three-three (not that likely – but there really is no other hope). So cross back to ♦A and lead a third diamond, counting the missing diamonds down from six (their initial number). They each follow three times, so there are no more left out. West wins the third round of the suit with ♦K (crashing East's ♦J), and probably plays another spade (nothing works better). Win ♠K and triumphantly cash ♦9, a promoted length winner. You can now take your remaining top spade, plus ♥A. Seven tricks and part-score made.

If you remember just one thing about ...

Bidding: Leave partner in his 1NT opener, with no five-card suit and up to 10 points.
Declaring: Don't panic in 1NT. Same as any other contract, look out for card-promotion opportunities (here, ♦Q).
Defending: Versus no-trumps, lead a long suit and keep plugging away at it.

Example D

Dealer South

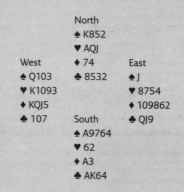

```
                  North
                  ♠ K852
                  ♥ AQJ
      West        ♦ 74         East
      ♠ Q103      ♣ 8532       ♠ J
      ♥ K1093                  ♥ 8754
      ♦ KQJ5                   ♦ 109862
      ♣ 107       South        ♣ QJ9
                  ♠ A9764
                  ♥ 62
                  ♦ A3
                  ♣ AK64
```

The bidding:

South	West	North	East
1♠	Pass	3♠ (i)	Pass
4♠ (ii)	End		

(i) 10–12 points (or a little less with compensating shape), plus four+ card support for partner's spades.

(ii) There being the 25 points for game (and aren't those aces lovely – aces are slightly undervalued at four points; jacks slightly overvalued at one).

The play:

West leads ♦K (showing ♦Q and denying ♦A) against your 4♠ game. You win ♦A, and there is no reason to delay drawing trumps. You cross to ♠K, and return to ♠A. East discards on the second round, meaning that the suit has (not unexpectedly) split three-one. Should you give West his ♠Q?

good to know
Especially in trump contracts, aces are slightly undervalued at four points; jacks slightly overvalued at one.

No – leave the master trump outstanding (the Rule of One). Why waste two of your trumps to get rid of a trump that's going to win a trick anyway? Instead try the heart finesse. Lead ♥2 to ♥3 and ♥J. Good – because West holds ♥K, ♥J is promoted. Now cross to ♣K and lead ♥6 to ♥9 and ♥Q. As expected, this card is also promoted (if East held ♥K he would presumably have beaten ♥J with ♥K on the first round). The winning heart finesse has dramatically improved matters, as you can now cash ♥A and discard ♦3. Next follow with a second club to ♣A and, with both opponents following (revealing a three-two split), you can give the opponents a third club. East wins ♣Q but you can trump his diamond return, and lead the promoted fourth-round length winner in clubs. You do not mind if West trumps with ♠Q – he must make this card at some stage. All you lose is ♠Q and ♣Q – 11 tricks and game made plus one.

If you remember just one thing about ...

Bidding: Support at the Three-level shows 10–12 points.
Declaring: Leave the master trump outstanding – the Rule of One.
Defending: The lead of an honour card shows the card immediately below and denies the card immediately above.

Example E

Dealer South

	North	
	♠ 10754	
	♥ A86	
West	♦ J53	East
♠ 9	♣ J65	♠ KJ6
♥ J92		♥ K1053
♦ Q742	South	♦ 10986
♣ AK1097	♠ AQ832	♣ 82
	♥ Q74	
	♦ AK	
	♣ Q43	

The bidding:

South	West	North	East
1♠	2♣ (i)	2♠ (ii)	Pass
3♠ (iii)	Pass	Pass (iv)	Pass

(i) West is worth the overcall – showing a good five-card suit (satisfying SQOT).

(ii) 6–9 points and support (could be just three cards for a single raise).

(iii) Inviting the spade game. In effect saying, 'Partner, you have shown me a bad hand. But I'm still interested in game (4♠). Do you have a good bad hand, or a bad bad hand?'

(iv) Bad bad hand. North is absolutely minimum, and flat as a pancake (not even a doubleton for trumping potential).

The play:

West leads the ace of clubs – ace from ace-king is the best lead of all – and East has the opportunity to signal whether he wants West to continue (with king and a third round). Because he does – having third-round control in the form of a doubleton, East plays ♣8 ('throw high means aye'). West duly continues with ♣K and a third club, East trumping (with ♠6). East switches to ♦10 – dummy's weakness – and you as declarer can afford to lose just one more trick.

Win ♦K and, needing to promote ♠Q via a finesse, cross to ♥A to lead ♠4. When East follows with ♠J, you try ♠Q. Good news! The finesse succeeds (the second player holding ♠K), and you now cash ♠A, felling his ♠K. Trumps drawn (did you count them in the best way – just focusing on the four missing cards?), you now need to promote ♥Q.

Cash ♦A (in case ♦Q falls), then lead over to ♠10 (even though the opposing trumps have been drawn, you must waste two of your trumps because it is the only way to reach dummy to lead towards ♥Q). Your ♥6 lead from dummy reaps the necessary reward. Because East holds ♥K, he cannot prevent your ♥Q from being promoted. If he plays ♥K, you play ♥7 and make ♥Q next time; if he plays low, you play ♥Q, and it wins the trick. You score five trumps (via a successful finesse against East's ♠K), ♦AK, ♥A and ♥Q (via a successful finesse against East's ♥K). Nine tricks and part-score made.

If you remember just one thing about ...

Bidding: Remember the Suit Quality Overcall Test (SQOT).
Declaring: When finessing, lead from the opposite hand to the card you are trying to promote.
Defending: When, against a trump contract, partner leads an ace (from ace-king), you should encourage by playing a high spot card when you have third-round control (i.e. the queen or a doubleton).

Example F

Dealer South

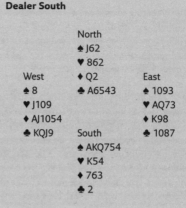

North
♠ J62
♥ 862
♦ Q2
♣ A6543

West
♠ 8
♥ J109
♦ AJ1054
♣ KQJ9

East
♠ 1093
♥ AQ73
♦ K98
♣ 1087

South
♠ AKQ754
♥ K54
♦ 763
♣ 2

The bidding:

South	West	North	East
1♠	2♦ (i)	2♠ (ii)	3♦ (iii)
3♠ (iv)	Pass (v)	Pass	Pass

(i) Five good cards – with a SQOT of eight.

(ii) A single major raise can be made without a fourth trump. To do so (even at the risk of playing a seven-card fit) is far better than passing (which has become an option – with at least six points – only because West's overcall gives South another bid without North having to speak), or bidding the nebulous 1NT (which North can't do here anyway as West overcalled 2♦).

(iii) Partner has at least five good diamonds. Admittedly the Three-level might be one beyond the level of the fit, but partner won't quibble. Support is always welcome news.

(iv) Facing 6–9 points (as advertised by the 2♠ bid), South knows he is well short of the 25 for game. But he has wonderful spades and feeble defensive

---

good to know

On competitive deals, where the high-card points are evenly split and each side has a good (eight- or nine-card) fit, the auction often ends with the highest-ranking suit winning the bidding at the Three-level.

---

prospects to a diamond contract (defending 3♠, his three top spades are certainly not going to live). It is imperative that he declare the deal (or push East–West overboard).

(v) With a sixth diamond, West would consider bidding on to 4♦.

The play:

In spite of his side bidding and supporting diamonds, it is very inadvisable to lead away from an ace. Instead West prefers to lead from his excellent club sequence, choosing the king (showing the queen and denying the ace). You, as declarer, view dummy and count seven top tricks – six trumps plus ♣A. You note that there is a suit in which dummy has fewer cards than you: diamonds. So you must delay drawing trumps, and plan to void dummy of diamonds, preparatory to trumping your third diamond in dummy.

Win ♣A and lead a diamond. The defence win and, seeing your strategy, promptly switch to a trump (trying to get rid of dummy's trumps). You win and lead a second diamond, thus voiding dummy of diamonds. East wins and leads a second trump, but you are in control. Win in hand, and trump your third diamond with dummy's last trump. Seven tricks have become eight. To make a ninth trick – and your contract – you need to promote ♥K. This involves a finesse – leading from the opposite hand to ♥K, and hoping the second player (here East) has ♥A. Conveniently you are currently in dummy – and there for the last time. So you lead ♥2 and, because East does indeed hold ♥A, watch him either rise with the card or not, and your ♥K is promoted. Nine tricks and game made.

Note that at no stage were you tempted to trump a club in your hand. This would not create any extra tricks because you have already counted six trumps. All you would do by trumping a club is find another way to make one of your low trumps that are bound to score a trick anyway – a pointless exercise.

If you remember just one thing about ...

Bidding: The single major raise only guarantees three-card support.

Declaring: In a trump contract, look for a suit in which dummy has fewer cards than you; if there is one, then delay drawing trumps and void yourself of that suit. Then trump your extra card(s) in dummy.

Defending: If you see declarer delaying drawing trumps and voiding the dummy of a short side-suit, lead trumps whenever you win the lead.

Example G

Dealer South

North
♠ 862
♥ K7
♦ AQJ42
♣ 876

West
♠ Q9754
♥ Q94
♦ 1095
♣ J10

East
♠ K103
♥ J832
♦ K7
♣ Q932

South
♠ AJ
♥ A1065
♦ 863
♣ AK54

The bidding:

South	West	North	East
1♥ (i)	Pass	2♦ (ii)	Pass
2NT (iii)	Pass	3NT (iv)	End

(i) South is balanced, but too strong to open 1NT. Instead he temporizes with a suit bid, planning to rebid no-trumps. In the recommended style, he chooses the higher-ranking suit.
(ii) Easy response of the longest suit at the lowest level. Take away ♥K, however, and North would lack the strength for a new suit at the Two-level (failing the Rule of 14). He would then respond the 'dustbin' 1NT.
(iii) 15–16 balanced.
(iv) Knowing the partnership has the 25 points for game.

The play:

West leads ♠5 – 'fourth highest' – and East must play ♠K – 'third hand high'. You, as declarer, win ♠A (perhaps you should not?) and, needing extra tricks from diamonds, lead ♦3 to ♦J. Sadly (for you) the finesse loses, ♦J losing to ♦K. Now East must return a second spade – but which one?

If East returns ♠3, he blocks the suit. Your ♠J loses to West's ♠Q, but a third spade is won perforce by East's ♠10. With no way to regain the lead, West 'goes to bed' with his two remaining length winners in spades, and the game makes. East must return ♠10 at Trick Three – top of two remaining (key play). West takes your ♠J with ♠Q, but his ♠9 is now the third-round spade master, and he is able to cash that card and follow with his two long spades. Down one – nothing you could do.

If you remember just one thing about …

Bidding: Open the higher-ranking of equal length suits (except 1♥ with precisely 4–4 in the majors).

Declaring: Don't despair when things look bleak. The opponents sometimes come to your rescue!

Defending: Lead top of a remaining doubleton (as you would an original doubleton). It is a key unblocking manoeuvre.

Example H

Dealer North

```
                    North
                    ♠ AQJ6
                    ♥ AKJ54
        West        ♦ KJ6        East
        ♠ 983       ♣ 7          ♠ 75
        ♥ 9763                   ♥ 82
        ♦ 2                      ♦ A9843
        ♣ Q10985    South        ♣ AJ43
                    ♠ K1042
                    ♥ Q10
                    ♦ Q1075
                    ♣ K62
```

The bidding:

South	West	North	East
		1♥	Pass
1♠ (i)	Pass	4♠ (ii)	End

(i) Showing four+ spades and six+ points.
(ii) Knows immediately that a fit is found (spades), and that the values for game are present.

The play:

West has a nasty surprise awaiting declarer – he leads ♦2. Only an ace from ace-king is superior to a side-suit singleton lead.

The lead of a singleton can succeed spectacularly, defeating a contract that looks ironclad when declarer first sees dummy. Here you as declarer think you have just to lose the two minor-suit aces. You are about to be disappointed.

East wins ♦2 lead (which cannot be a doubleton, as West would lead top from two) with ♦A, and returns ♦3. West trumps and, hoping East holds ♣A (you might recall the Suit Preference Signal: when leading for partner to trump, the lead of a low card asks for the return of the lower-ranking suit, here clubs), duly switches to a club. Bingo! East wins ♣A, and a third diamond is trumped by West. You can win any return, draw trumps, and claim the remainder. But the devastating defence has brought you down one.

If you remember just one thing about ...

Bidding: If you know what trumps are, and that you have the values for game, you should go straight there.

Declaring: Don't count your chickens ... Bad things can happen to even the most ironclad-looking contract.

Defending: A singleton lead is only surpassed in attractiveness by an ace from ace-king.

Example 1

Dealer South

	North	
	♠ 109864	
	♥ K75	
West	♦ AKJ2	East
♠ 732	♣ 7	♠ 5
♥ QJ109		♥ A62
♦ 10		♦ 97543
♣ AK653	South	♣ 10942
	♠ AKQJ	
	♥ 843	
	♦ Q86	
	♣ QJ8	

The bidding:

South	West	North	East
1♠ (i)	Pass (ii)	4♠ (iii)	End

(i) Too strong for 1NT.

(ii) Clubs not strong enough for a Two-level overcall. On a bad day, you might win just two tricks. Much better to hold KQJ109 (less points but a guarantee of four tricks).

(iii) What a wonderful hand in support of spades. The point-count might suggest bidding a non-forcing 3♠, but the fifth trump and singleton club (worth about three points) make North's hand a clear 4♠ bid. Not that you as his partner are about to make it ...

The play:

The best lead against a trump contract is ace from ace-king and this deal perfectly illustrates why. West might be tempted to lead his singleton diamond (we have seen how effective a singleton lead can be). Singleton leads can work out fantastically, partner winning the lead and leading a second round for you to trump. But declarer often wins the lead, draws your trumps, and the defence have lost the initiative. The reason why ace from ace-king is a better lead is that it keeps all the leader's options open. After seeing dummy, he can continue with the king, switch to his singleton, or even try a third alternative.

On this occasion a look at dummy after the recommended lead of ♣A tells West neither to carry on with clubs (dummy being void), nor to switch to his singleton diamond (dummy's diamonds being so strong). Instead he should hope for his partner to hold ♥A (his only real chance of beating the game), and switch to ♥Q. Bingo! You as declarer are now stuffed. If you withhold dummy's king, ♥Q will win, and ♥J will follow. If you cover with ♥K, East wins ♥A and ♥6 return sees West score two more winners. Down one.

Note that on an initial diamond lead, you can draw trumps and cash diamonds, discarding a heart loser on dummy's fourth-round diamond winner. In this way you hold your losers to one club and two hearts – game made.

If you remember just one thing about ...

Bidding: Upgrade a supporting hand with a singleton. It is worth about three extra points when you have at least four-card trump support.
Declaring: Take defeat gracefully. Congratulate your opponents when they make a fine defence.
Defending: Ace from ace-king – Andrew's favourite lead – gives you a free look at dummy, and thereby keeps all your options open.

Example J

Dealer South

	North	
	♠ J8532	
	♥ KQ64	
West	♦ K105	East
♠ Q9	♣ 5	♠ 7
♥ A108		♥ 97532
♦ 8763		♦ AQJ
♣ AJ83	South	♣ Q976
	♠ AK1064	
	♥ J	
	♦ 942	
	♣ K1042	

The bidding:

South	West	North	East
1♠ (i)	Pass	3♠ (ii)	Pass
Pass (iii)	Pass		

(i) Only just an opening bid, but remember the Rule of 20: open when your points added to the number of cards in your two longest suits reaches 20. Admittedly (and dubiously) this is giving full value to the singleton ♥J, but those spades look great, don't they?

(ii) Closer to 4♠ than 2♠, even though there are just nine points. The singleton club and the fifth trump are huge.

(iii) Holding an absolute minimum, South has to turn down the invitation.

The play:

What is the worst opening lead against a trump contract? Right – leading away from an ace. This deal illustrates why.

Say West leads a club or a heart (away from the ace). You as declarer win the trick, draw trumps by cashing ♠AK, and lose at most three diamonds and the ♥/♣A that West didn't lead away from. West will never score the ace he led away from because declarer/dummy will trump. Nine tricks and part-score made.

If West, however, finds an alternative lead, which by a process of elimination can only be a diamond (he can hardly lead a trump, holding as he does ♠Q9), then the defence will prevail. West therefore leads ♦8 (lead 'high for hate'). You as declarer correctly see no point in rising with dummy's ♦K, because West would not lead away from an ace at Trick One to a trump contract. You play dummy's ♦5. East now wins with ♦J, the cheaper of his ♦QJ sequence.

At Trick Two East must now refrain from continuing diamonds, retaining ♦AQ over dummy's ♦K. He can switch to any suit, but dummy's strong hearts make ♣6 look best (voiding dummy is hardly attractive, but it is the lesser of evils).

West covers your forlorn ♣K with ♣A, and leads a second diamond (he knows his partner holds ♦AQ, because ♦J won the first trick – you see why playing the cheaper of equals gives more information). East beats dummy's ♦10 with ♦Q, cashes ♦A, and West must score ♥A. Down one.

If you remember just one thing about ...

Bidding: Remember the Rule of 20 for opener.
Declaring: Assume that an opening leader to a trump contract does not have the ace of the suit led. A corollary of ...
Defending: Do not lead away from an ace at Trick One to a trump contract.

4 Development

In this chapter you'll learn some advanced strategies in the bidding, including doubles, slams and basic conventions, and more techniques for evaluating a bridge hand. As before, prior to learning these new skills make sure you have plenty of practice. An instructive exercise is to play all four hands yourself. When you're ready, you'll enjoy developing your game, taking it to a stimulating and challenging new level.

Double

'Double' is arguably the most useful bid in bridge. Two types of double are used: their meanings are opposite so it is vital to know which one your partner has bid. Like any other bid, three passes following a double are required to end the auction.

must know

• A penalty double is used when you think your opponents will fail to reach their contract. You 'double' the final contract, which means you get extra penalty points (more than double points) if your opponents fail to fulfil their contract, but they get double points if they succeed (see pp. 224–5 for scoring doubles).

• A take-out double is used to ask your partner to communicate to you his preferred suits, with the aim of finding a viable contract for your side.

• For both types you say: 'double'.

Two types of double

As we've seen in chapter 3, the literal meaning of double is 'I don't think my opponents will make their contract'. Such 'penalty' doubles are used to double a bid made by an opponent when your partner has already bid, or when doubling no-trumps.

The other type of double, for 'take-out', is used when your partner hasn't yet made a positive bid (a bid other than a pass), it's aim being to ask your partner to make a bid and to find a viable contract for your side.

Take-out double

If you double an opening bid before your partner has made a positive bid, you are, in effect, asking your partner to 'take-out' your double, i.e. switch to any of the other suits so that your side can find a fit. Your partner's bid effectively cancels the double.

The requirements for a take-out double are as follows:

> **S**upport (3+ cards) for all of the unbid suits
> **O**pening points (or more) in your hand
> **S**hortage (0, 1, 2 cards) in the opposing suit(s) ('SOS')

These are the strict criteria for a take-out double, but perhaps more importantly is a feel for what the doubling hand should look like: it should be a promising-looking collection that is unhappy defending the current bid and wants partner to choose any of the other suits. Don't double if you're only interested in one suit – simply bid that suit; and don't double if you're happy defending the current contract.

Let's consider which of the following hands should make a (take-out) double following an opening of 1♥ by your right-hand opponent:

(a)	(b)	(c)	(d)	(e)
♠ AQ94	♠ 32	♠ A2	♠ QJ942	♠ AK76
♥ 5	♥ KJ6	♥ KJ10983	♥ A3	♥ 72
♦ KJ76	♦ AQ32	♦ AQ	♦ K74	♦ AKQ6
♣ AJ64	♣ AQJ7	♣ 532	♣ A32	♣ KQ10

(a) You have the perfect shape for a take-out double – 4441 with a singleton in the suit opened – showing how a normally awkward hand pattern can suddenly describe itself very accurately in one bid. You have good support for any unbid suit your partner cares to choose. How nice to have this take-out double available, because you can't overcall for the lack of a five-card suit. Bid: double.

(b) You have a better alternative. Firstly, a double here is flawed because you need more than a small doubleton in the other major (i.e. spades, the highest ranking suit). Secondly, you have a perfect hand for a 1NT overcall (15–19 points, balanced, with a 'stopper' in the opponents' suit, hearts – i.e. a way of stopping them run through the suit). Bid: 1NT.

(c) You don't expect them to make 1♥, but to double would have the reverse meaning, showing short hearts and support for the other suits. Better to pass and hope they'll bid more hearts. Bid: pass.

(d) It's tempting to double, but the fifth card in the other major is too valuable to hide – failing to overcall 1♠ could easily see you miss a 5–3 spade fit. Bid: 1♠.

(e) This is similar to (a): a perfect double. Note that you can never be too strong to double. Bid: double.

Responding to a take-out double

If your partner makes a take-out double it effectively forces you to respond (unless the intervening player bids – see p. 130). Your response strategy is summarized below. As you can see, it's based on the strength of your hand. Do remember to jump the bidding with nine+ points. Bidding at the lowest level is consistent with no points at all – you have been forced to speak. Note also that you should bid an unbid major in preference to an unbid minor: partly because it's higher-scoring, and partly because your partner is more likely to make a take-out double if he holds four cards in unbid majors (more than four cards in minors).

Strategies for responding to a take-out double

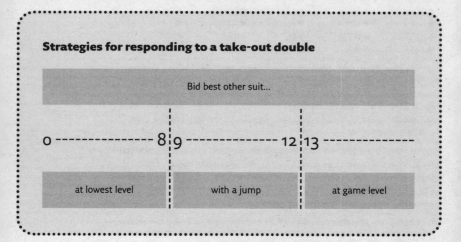

Bid best other suit...

0 ----------- 8	9 ------------ 12	13 ------------
at lowest level	with a jump	at game level

Note that when responding to the double of an opening bid, it's helpful to think of your partner as holding a 12-point, 4441-hand with a singleton in opener's suit. This is a guide only: she may have more points (there's no upper limit), or her hand may be less shape-suitable than this.

Let's look at what your response should be when your partner doubles a 1♦ opener (and the next hand passes) if you hold each of the following hands:

(a)	(b)	(c)
♠ 95	♠ 9832	♠ AK974
♥ K932	♥ Q5	♥ 63
♦ 543	♦ 108543	♦ Q62
♣ K1095	♣ 83	♣ KJ3

(a) Bid 1♥. Hearts is preferable to clubs because it's a major suit scoring more points than clubs (a minor), and, crucially, it can be bid at a level lower.

(b) Bid 1♠. You've been forced to bid a suit other than diamonds. It may seem tempting to pass (making diamonds trumps), but assuming your partner has the classic take-out double shape (4441 with a singleton in their diamonds) the spade contract should work despite your meagre point count. Also, 1♦ doubled will play well for the opposition – another reason to stop diamonds being trumps.

(c) Bid 4♠. Don't simply bid 1♠ – your partner may think you have hand (b), or worse. Your partner has guaranteed three spades and opening points, so you can bid 4♠: there's a known spade fit, plus the points for game.

Now consider what you would bid with the hands in the next example. The bidding began 1♥-double-pass (your left-hand opponent opened 1♥, your partner doubled, and your right-hand opponent passed).

(d)	(e)	(f)
♠ 863	♠ K6	♠ K864
♥ J543	♥ J86	♥ 864
♦ 74	♦ AQ975	♦ K8
♣ 9754	♣ 643	♣ AJ96

(d) Despite your weak hand you can't pass, so bid your best other suit, 2♣. Yuk – but at least your partner knows you've been forced to speak, and that you may have a hand as bad as this (up to a maximum of eight points).

(e) Bid 3♦. By jumping the bidding, you show 9–12 points.

(f) Bid 2♠, showing your 9–12 points, and preferring the major suit at the Two level to the minor at the Three level.

Responding to opener – cancelling the double

When your partner opens One-of-a-suit, and your right-hand opponent doubles, this shouldn't affect your response strategy – just carry on with your bid. However, note that your bid, should you make one, has the effect of cancelling the double (and its threat of penalties or promise of extra points), thus removing the obligation on the partner of the doubler to speak.

Move back into the seat of the responder to the double. Let's consider what you should bid with the hands (d), (e) and (f) in the previous example, after your partner's double has been cancelled.

The bidding so far is: 1♣-double-1♥ (your left-hand opponent opened 1♣, your partner doubled and your right-hand opponent responded 1♥ – thus removing your obligation to bid).

(d) You should be happy to pass.

(e) and (f) With both hands you should bid – with a jump to show their 9–12 point range. With (e) bid 3♦ and with (f) bid 2♠. Just because you don't have to bid, it doesn't mean you should always pass. If ♣A was ♣2 in hand (f), you could still – very comfortably – compete with a bid of 1♠ over right-hand opponent's 1♥.

Take-out or penalty?

The penalty double (where you think the opposition are unlikely to make their contract) is radically different in meaning from the take-out double, and yet the same bid is used. Things would be easier if you could say 'take-out double' or 'penalty double', but unfortunately you must simply say 'double'. Clearly it's vital there is no confusion between the two. The chart on the next page shows how to decide between the two doubles. In essence, the rule is: until your partner has made a positive bid, a double of a suit bid (though not a no-trump bid) is for take-out. This is basically true (within reason) on any round of the bidding, and at any level.

Is your double for take-out or penalty?

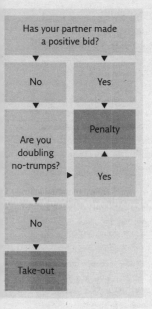

must know

In general, a double is for take-out if it is a double of a suit bid (not a double of a no-trump bid) and the partner of the doubler has not yet bid.

Now consider whether the doubles (bid by you as South) in the following auctions are doubles for take-out or penalties, and what your hand might look like in each case:

	South	West	North	East
(a)		1♣	pass	1♥
	double			
(b)				1♥
	double	2♥	pass	pass
	double			
(c)		1♥	pass	4♥
	double			
(d)	1♥	2♦	pass	pass
	double			
(e)			1♥	2♦
	double			

(a) Your double is for take-out, because your partner (North) hasn't made a positive bid. In effect you're asking your partner to bid one of the two unbid suits (i.e. you are 'take-out doubling' clubs and hearts). Your hand might be: ♠ AQ105, ♥ 75, ♦ KQ973, ♣ K5.

(b) You double twice. Your first is a take-out double. This is cancelled by West's 2♥ bid so North, presumably very weak, is free to pass. Your second double, also for take-out (your partner having not bid), says in effect, 'I have more than a minimum opener and really want you to bid'. Your hand might be: ♠ AKJ6, ♥ 5, ♦ AQ97, ♣ KJ65.

(c) Another take-out double (even at this high level of bidding), because your partner hasn't made a positive bid. Your hand will look something like this: ♠ AJ98, ♥-, ♦ KQ862, ♣ A1087. Note that, while your partner is expected to take-out the double, she can, at such a high level, opt to convert the take-out double into penalties by passing at her next bid (she wouldn't do this at lower levels). If her hand was ♠ 64, ♥ QJ9, ♦ 7532, ♣ 9632, she'd be best passing than raising a level (e.g. to 5♣) as she's unlikely to make eleven tricks in a minor suit, whereas she will probably score four tricks in defence – enough to a beat a 4♥ contract.

(d) Another take-out double because North hasn't yet made a positive bid (just because you've already bid doesn't alter this fact). You'll have an above-minimum opening hand, something like: ♠ AJ95, ♥ AQ752, ♦ 6, ♣ KQ10. Note that your second-round double is cheaper than bidding 2♠ (which would force your partner to bid 3♥ to give a preference back to the first suit). It also allows for clubs to be trumps.

(e) This is a penalty double – because your partner has bid. You'll have a decent hand, no great fit for your partner's hearts (or else you'd support her suit) and, crucially, good diamonds. Something like: ♠ A32, ♥ 5, ♦ QJ863, ♣ K963.

Useful tip

To make a penalty double at low levels (at the One, Two or Three levels in the bidding), you need good trumps (strong cards in the opposition's trump suit). Not so at high levels of bidding (a level of four and above), where high-card points outside the trump suit will suffice.

Low-level penalty doubles

If your partner opens One-of-a-suit and your right-hand opponent overcalls in another suit, you should make a penalty double when you have:

- A very good holding in the overcalled suit.
- No fit for your partner.
- At least half the pack of points between the partnership (i.e. 20+ points).

Use this chart to see if your holding in the over-caller's suit is strong enough for a double:

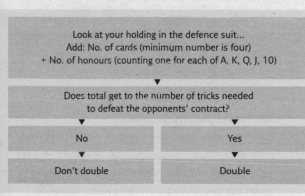

Penalty doubling at low levels – are your trumps good enough?

Look at your holding in the defence suit...
Add: No. of cards (minimum number is four)
+ No. of honours (counting one for each of A, K, Q, J, 10)

▼

Does total get to the number of tricks needed to defeat the opponents' contract?

▼   ▼

No   Yes

▼   ▼

Don't double   Double

Now consider what you should bid with the following hands. Your partner has opened 1♥, and your right-hand opponent has overcalled 2♦.

(a)	(b)	(c)	(d)
♠ Q2	♠ Q63	♠ K53	♠ A76
♥ J1073	♥ 3	♥ 73	♥ 72
♦ A7654	♦ KJ84	♦ Q98532	♦ K1073
♣ 53	♣ A9753	♣ Q5	♣ A763

(a) 2♥. You have a heart fit, so must support your partner's bid. (Your diamonds are probably too weak for a penalty double anyway, given that you have just one likely winner, the ace.)

(b) Double. Your trumps are good enough, and you suspect a 'misfit' – where neither side will make much of anything.

(c) Pass. You have inadequate overall strength for a double. Be happy the opponents are playing in diamonds; you don't want to tip them off to switch suits.

(d) Double. You have diamonds that satisfy the penalty double criteria, the balance of the points, and a likely misfit.

Scoring doubles is covered on pp. 224–5, but for now it's worth noting that if your double in (b) and (d) backfires – and the opponents make their doubled contract – it gives them a score of twice the normal contract score (i.e. 40 x 2 = 80). However, even if you 'double your opponents into game' (so their score reaches 100, i.e. game points), the odd such 'disaster' is more than compensated for by the 300, 500 or 800 bonuses awarded to you when things go your way.

High level penalty doubles

If you've bid to game and expect to make it, yet your opponents have bid over you, they're almost bound to be 'sacrificing'. This means they're expecting to go down but lose fewer points for failure than you'd

eceive making your game. In these situations you
must double – even if your trumps are poor. You
eed very few tricks to defeat them, and they should
ome from outside trumps.

Let's consider the following auction:

West	North	East	South
	1NT	Pass	3♠
4♥	4♠	5♥	?

When you (as South) jump to 3♠, you show game
values with precisely five spades. Surprisingly,
your opponents now bid up to 5♥. With each of
the following hands, what should you now bid?

(a)	(b)	(c)	(d)
♠ AQ972	♠ KQ1063	♠ KQ853	♠ AJ976
♥ 3	♥ –	♥ J3	♥ 2
♦ A754	♦ KJ1084	♦ A532	♦ K973
♣ Q53	♣ QJ3	♣ Q5	♣ A63

(a), (c) and (d) should all double – 'the Five level
belongs to the opponents' (i.e. don't bid 'five over
five'). But a conflicting motto, 'Bid one more with
a void', makes hand (b) a reasonable 5♠ bid.

Doubles of no-trumps

Doubles of no-trumps are always for penalty (it
would make no sense to double no-trumps for take-
out, because there's no suit to take out). The most
important situation is the double of a 1NT opener.
This shows any hand with 16+ points (i.e. a little
better than the 1NT opener's hand), even an
unbalanced one with a long suit. The points you
gain from defending 1NT doubled will probably far
exceed the points you gain from making a part-
score (even a game).

must know
Having more high-card
points than your
opponents doesn't mean
you have to declare.
You'll often win more
points by doubling your
opponents instead.

Doubling a 1NT opener

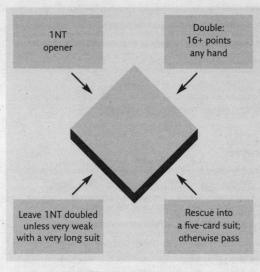

1NT
opener

Double:
16+ points
any hand

Leave 1NT doubled
unless very weak
with a very long suit

Rescue into
a five-card suit;
otherwise pass

Let's consider what you should bid if your right-hand opponent opens 1NT:

(a)	(b)	(c)	(d)
♠ AQ9752	♠ J	♠ A53	♠ KJ6
♥ A10	♥ Q108653	♥ KJ73	♥ A2
♦ KJ74	♦ A974	♦ AQ	♦ AK73
♣ A	♣ AQ	♣ A1085	♣ 9763

(a) Double, showing 16+ points.

(b) 2♥, showing a good suit (SQOT), but a maximum of 15 points (with more points you'd double).

(c) Double.

(d) Pass – not quite enough points to double.

Note:
(i) The partner of the 1NT opener should react with trepidation to a penalty double on his right, as he's almost bound to be weak. If he has a five-card suit (or longer), he must make a weakness take-out

must know
Doubling 1NT shows any hand with 16+ points, whereas a suit overcall shows a hand with a maximum of 15 points.

into that suit. With no five-card suit, he can only pass and hope his partner won't suffer too much. (ii) The partner of the doubler is in a better position. Assuming the bidding has gone 1NT, double, pass, he should almost always pass, unless his hand is very weak (0–3 points) and unbalanced, in which case he should take-out into his five-card suit.

Redouble

This rarely used bid can only be made if an opponent doubles you. Redoubling in effect says, 'You may have thought you own the deal. You don't – we do!' If a contract ends up redoubled, then the resulting score is twice that of a doubled contract (see p. 225 for scoring redoubles).

You can survive perfectly well without ever redoubling. In practice, the only time you are likely to choose to use this bid is when your partner's opening bid of One-of-a-suit is doubled for take-out by the opposing side. Redoubling here implies you have around 10+ points and a 'flattish' hand with no great fit for your partner or good suit of your own. It announces ownership of the deal to your partner, who may otherwise be put off after his opening bid has been take-out doubled.

see p. 225

must know
After an opponent doubles your bid, you or your partner may then redouble (say 'Redouble'). A redouble increases the points scored for successfully fulfilling the contract, and increases the penalties for failing to fulfil the contract, yet further than a double.

Useful tip
Generally, it is inadvisable to redouble a penalty double – if your opponents think you are going down (unlikely to make your contract), they are probably right.

Bidding a slam

Up to this point, our jackpot in the bidding has been to bid for game: 3NT, 4♥, 4♠, 5♣ and 5♦. As you play more, however, you'll gain the confidence and technique to aim even higher, with a 'slam'.

Grand slams and small slams

There are big scoring bonuses for bidding and making 12 tricks on a deal, a 'small slam', and there are possibilities for doing this about one deal in 15. The ultimate jackpot in bridge is to bid and make all 13 tricks in one deal, known as a 'grand slam'.

To attempt such a tall order is a big gamble, because to fail by even one trick sees you score nothing, and lose the opportunity to make a game contract that was probably easily available. But the lure is great because of the big bonuses to be made, as shown here:

	Not vulnerable (you have not won a game)	Vulnerable (you are one game towards a rubber*)
Small Slam ('Six of something')	500	750
Grand Slam ('Seven of something')	1000	1500

*a rubber = best of three games

Scoring bonuses for bidding slams

The guideline number of partnership high-card points needed for a grand slam is 37 (out of 40). Pretty rare! My advice is to leave the bidding of grand slams to professionals. If I use the word 'slam' from now on, assume I'm talking about the much more attainable small slam.

Bidding slam in no-trumps

The guideline number of partnership high-card points for game in no-trumps is 25. The number needed for a small slam is 33.

Let's consider what you should bid if your partner opens 1NT:

(a)	(b)	(c)
♠ AQ2	♠ AJ7	♠ A103
♥ A104	♥ KQ5	♥ KQ7
♦ AK74	♦ A974	♦ AQ98
♣ KJ9	♣ KJ8	♣ A108

(a) You know that the partnership has 33 points, so jump straight to 6NT (12 tricks needed for a slam).

(b) You have a very good hand, but, even if your partner has 14 points for his 1NT (and he can't have more), there aren't quite the 33 points needed for slam. And there's no point going higher than game if you know you can't make slam. Simply bid 3NT, expecting your partner to make ten or eleven tricks, but probably not 12.

(c) With 19 points (and decent ones – look at the good 'intermediate cards', i.e. tens and nines), your hand is borderline for a slam. If your partner has a maximum 1NT, the values for slam will be present. If he's minimum, game will probably be the limit. You need to make a slam-invitational bid: 4NT. Because you have bid beyond game, your partner will know you're interested in slam.

Note: The 4NT slam-invitational bid says to your partner: 'pass with a minimum, bid 6NT with a maximum'.

must know
• The partnership high-card point guideline of 33 for a small slam is an especially accurate guide in no-trumps.
• If you want your partner to know you are interested in slam (you have invitational values to 6NT), then make a slam invitational bid of 4NT over your partner's no-trump opener.

**The rewards for slams
are so high that it is
worth considering a
slam whenever both
partners hold
excessively strong
hands – with values far
exceeding those needed
for game. However,
contracting for 12 or
more tricks is risky and
should only be done if
you are confident you
can win them.**

Now consider what you should respond after the
following bidding: you open 1NT and your partner
jumps to 4NT (no-trump slam invite):

(d)	(e)	(f)
♠ KJ2	♠ A97	♠ QJ3
♥ A4	♥ AJ5	♥ K108
♦ QJ74	♦ K974	♦ A10982
♣ K1095	♣ 1084	♣ K9

(d) Bid 6NT. You have a maximum 1NT opener –
so you must accept the slam invite.

(e) Pass. You have a minimum 1NT hand.

(f) Bid 6NT. You're in the middle of the point-
range, but what a 13-point hand! Good
intermediates and a five-card suit.

Bidding slams in trump suits

Although 33 partnership high-card points is still a
useful guideline, big fits and shortages (i.e. singletons
and voids) can compensate for the lack of high cards
when bidding slams in trump suits. Frequently a slam
can be made with fewer than 33 points, sometimes far
fewer, making the chance of a slam coming your way
rather more than you may expect. However, because
losing a slam respresents a waste of a game you could
easily have won otherwise, it's best when beginning at
bridge to attempt only those slams that you believe
are likely to succeed.

Useful tip
If you want to practise your slam bidding, take out all the twos, threes,
fours and fives from a pack and deal two hands from the remainder.

140 | Beginner's Guide to Bridge

The most famous deal in bridge history

In this celebrated deal, the East hand was originally 'dealt' (presumably a set-up job) to the Duke of Cumberland in the days of whist. His opponents goaded him into betting that he wouldn't make a single trick with clubs as trumps. Reputedly he lost £20,000 (a lot of money in the eighteenth century) when his opponents chalked up all 13 tricks.

Ian Fleming then used the deal in his book *Moonraker* (1955), featuring James Bond. Somewhat disappointingly for bridge players, it appeared only fleetingly in the 1979 film of the book.

Here it is:

```
                    North ('M')
                    ♠ 10987
                    ♥ 6543
West (Meyer)        ♦ -            East (Drax)
♠ 65432             ♣ 76532        ♠ AKQJ
♥ 109072                           ♥ AKQJ
♦ J109                             ♦ AK
♣ -                                ♣ KJ9
                    South (Bond)
                    ♠ -
                    ♥ -
                    ♦ Q8765432
                    ♣ AQ1084
```

After much posturing and raising of stakes between James Bond (South) and Drax (the 'baddie', East), Bond then 'deals' – using sleight of hand and a handkerchief, he substitutes the rigged deal – and opens the bidding: 7♣. After two passes, East doubles, South redoubles, then West (the hapless Meyer) leads ♦J. Dummy (the loyal 'M') tables his wares, whereupon the declarer (Bond) trumps the diamond in dummy (East following with ♦K), then leads ♣3 and beats East's ♣9 with his ♣10. He trumps a second diamond (bringing down East's ♦A), then plays a trump to East's ♣J and his ♣Q. He cashes ♣A felling East's ♣K, and runs through his tricks in diamonds (starting with ♦Q). Redoubled grand slam made.

An apoplectic Drax leaves the table with the words, 'I owe about £15,000. I will accept Meyer's addition'. On his way out he whispers in Bond's ear, 'I should spend the money hurriedly, Commander Bond'.

The deal may have been rigged – but it does illustrate the point: you don't necessarily need 33 points for slam in a trump suit.

The Blackwood convention

A 'convention' in bridge is a bid whose meaning is not connected to the suit mentioned in the bid (or no-trumps). 'Blackwood' is perhaps the most universally played convention. Two other conventions you will meet in a social setting are the 2♣ opener and 'Stayman' – see pp. 158 and 164.

see pp. 158 and 164

must know

The Blackwood convention is a bid of 4NT which asks your partner how many aces they hold. It is used if you are contemplating bidding a slam.

The Blackwood convention

When to use 'Blackwood'

When contemplating bidding a slam, it's imperative that the partnership holds all, or all but one, of the four aces. You won't make a small slam (all but one of the 13 tricks) if the opponents possess two aces (unless there's a void). It was because of the importance of the number of aces in slam bidding that US player Easley Blackwood invented the Blackwood convention (otherwise known as the '4NT ace-asking convention') way back in 1933. The bid and its responses are summarized below:

A bid of 4NT, when preceded by a suit bid, asks partner how many aces they hold	
Replies	5♣: Zero (or four) aces
	5♦: One ace
	5♥: Two aces
	5♠: Three aces

The 4NT bidder, to be consistent with her decision to go 'slamming via Blackwood', should only opt out if your reply to Blackwood indicates there are two or more missing aces: she should bid six of the agreed trump suit when the partnership has either three or four aces, but sign off in five of the trump suit when the partnership is missing two aces (to which you, her partner, should then pass).

If your reply indicates that all the aces are held, and your partner is interested in going for a grand slam (this is rare), she can bid 5NT to ask for kings – the replies are the same as for aces but one level higher. (Like bidding grand slams I'd advise against using this adjunct to the 4NT ace-ask.)

Let's see how Blackwood works in practice. Suppose your partner opens 1♥, you raise to 4♥, and your partner now bids 4NT (i.e. Blackwood). What should you reply with the following hands?

(a)	(b)	(c)
♠ 2	♠ AJ7	♠ KQ32
♥ AJ94	♥ J9532	♥ J1084
♦ AJ74	♦ KQ4	♦ KJ102
♣ Q1095	♣ Q4	♣ K

(a) Bid 5♥ (you have two aces).

(b) Bid 5♦ (you have one ace).

(c) Bid 5♣ (you have no aces).

Now consider what you should bid (as the 4NT bidder) if your partner replies 5♦ (i.e. he has one ace). The bidding so far: you opened 1♠, partner jumped to 4♠, you bid 4NT, and partner replied 5♦.

(a)	(b)	(c)
♠ AKJ32	♠ AKJ876	♠ AJ975
♥ 4	♥ A	♥ Q86
♦ KQJ74	♦ KQ974	♦ AKQ
♣ KQ	♣ 10	♣ J2

(a) You should sign off in 5♠ – which your partner must respect. Two aces are missing.

(b) Bid 6♠. Your only loser should be the one missing ace.

(c) This is a trap. With such a flat hand, you weren't strong enough to go slamming. You should have passed 4♠.

When not to use Blackwood

Here are three common scenarios where it would be a mistake to use Blackwood:

- You hold three or four aces in your own hand, so are not worried about your partner's number of aces. Assuming you're going to go for slam, simply jump to six of the trump suit yourself.
- Your partner's reply could take you beyond the safety of five of the trump suit. This applies when trumps are a minor suit (clubs or diamonds).
- You hold a void. It won't help you to know how many aces your partner has; you need to know which ones they are (only sophisticated 'cue-bidding' tools will help here – which are beyond the scope of this book).

Consider the following excellent hands. Your thoughts may well turn to the 6♣ slam, but which hands are suitable for the Blackwood 4NT ace-ask? You opened the bidding with 1♣, and your partner responded 3♣.

(a)	(b)	(c)	(d)
♠ KQ109	♠ 5	♠ QJ8	♠ AKJ3
♥ AQ	♥ AQ	♥ KJ9	♥ 5
♦ 10	♦ KQ63	♦ A10	♦ A6
♣ AK10842	♣ KQJ864	♣ AKJ85	♣ AK9863

(a) Yes – perfect for the Blackwood 4NT ace-ask. If your partner replies 5♣, you should pass (two aces are missing); if your partner replies 5♦, you can bid 6♣ and hope to lose just the one missing ace.

(b) No, you don't have enough aces. (If your partner replied 5♦ to your 4NT ace-ask, you'd know that two aces were missing from the partnership but you'd be stuck, unable to revert to 5♣. Instead of bidding 4NT, you should simply settle for a jump to 5♣.

(c) No, your hand is too balanced. If your partner did have one ace (replying 5♦ to your 4NT), and you ended up in 6♣, this could easily be a terrible slam (the opponents could have ♣AK and more). Better to settle for 3NT.

(d) No, there's no need for Blackwood here, as you have sufficient aces yourself. Your hand is so powerful that you should simply jump to 6♣.

> **must know**
> To be safe using Blackwood when clubs are trumps, you personally (not your partner) need two aces; when diamonds are trumps, you personally need (at least) one ace.

4NT: the two meanings

So far we've seen two uses for this bid. Bidding no-trump slams, it's an invitation based on point count (see pp. 139–40); bidding trump slams, it's a Blackwood 'ace-ask'. The chart below makes the distinction clear.

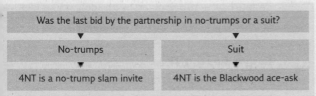

Was the last bid by the partnership in no-trumps or a suit?	
▼	▼
No-trumps	Suit
▼	▼
4NT is a no-trump slam invite	4NT is the Blackwood ace-ask

Is 4NT the Blackwood ace-ask or a no-trump slam invite?

Opening above the One level

In chapter 3 we looked at opening bids at the One level, essentially showing a hand worth 12–19 points. Here we'll look at cases where you have a stronger hand and open at the Two level (leaving 2♣ until p. 158); then cases where you have a weaker hand with a very long suit and can open at the Three or Four level.

(leaving 2♣ until p. 158)

> **must know**
>
> You should open the bidding at the Two level if you have a hand with 20 or more points (half the pack's points).

Opening 2NT

This opening bid shows a balanced hand with 20–22 points. Just occasionally you may open 2NT and be 'semi-balanced', e.g. 5422, or 6322 with a six-card club suit (see p. 175). The bid 2NT is the only Two-level opener that is non-forcing (i.e. your partner is allowed to pass). All the others are forcing for at least one round.

Here are some examples of 2NT openers:

(a)	(b)	(c)
♠ 63	♠ AKJ85	♠ KQ
♥ AKJ7	♥ K4	♥ AQ
♦ AJ105	♦ AQJ	♦ KJ97
♣ AK5	♣ K108	♣ AQ1086

In (a), you'd open 2NT despite your poor spades. In (b), you'd open 2NT despite your good five-card major (your hand is balanced). In (c), you'd open 2NT despite having two doubletons (the doubletons look good, and you have no better alternative).

Responding to 2NT

Even though opener is much stronger than responder, it's responder who now takes charge after

the opening bid. This is because responder knows
more about opener's hand than opener knows about
responder's.

Strategies for responding to a 2NT opener

Zone	No Game	Go for Game	Invite Slam	Go for Slam
points	0 -------- 3	4 -------- 10	11 ------- 12	13 --------
Strategy	Pass (there is no weakness take-out bid)	No five (+) card major: bid 3NT Five-card major: bid 3♥/♠ Six-card major: bid 4♥/♠	Balanced: bid 4NT	Five-card major: bid 3♥/♠ Six-card suit: bid Six-of-suit

Let's consider what you should respond to your partner's 2NT opener with each of the following hands:

(a)	(b)	(c)
♠ 4	♠ 2	♠ KQ10432
♥ K109742	♥ 964	♥ AQ2
♦ J105	♦ J9732	♦ Q32
♣ 985	♣ J983	♣ 9

(a) You're in the game zone (at worst, a point short, but the shape and length of your hand more than compensate). You know there's a heart fit – your partner must have at least two for his balanced bid. So jump to 4♥. Your partner knows you're in charge so won't bid more.

(b) You're in the part-score zone, but unfortunately there's no weakness take-out over 2NT, so you can't rescue into 3♦. Pass.

(c) This is a good hand to hold facing a 2NT opener. You know the values for slam are present, and there's a spade fit. Jump to 6♠. If you are worried that your opponents may have two aces, check your points: you have (at least) 33 points, leaving the opponents with at most seven points between them, which would make two aces impossible (at four points each).

Useful tip
Never lose sight of the fact that high-card points are only meant to be a guide. Bridge is a game about tricks.

Opening 2♦, 2♥, 2♠

These opening bids show:

- Strong, unbalanced hands with good five or usually six cards in the bid suit.
- 20-22 points; occasionally slightly less with a fine-looking hand and a six-card suit; never more (or you'd open 2♣ – see p. 158).

Let's consider what you should open with the following hands:

(a)	(b)	(c)
♠ AQJ1084	♠ 2	♠ 2
♥ AQ	♥ AQJ97	♥ Q9
♦ K73	♦ AKJ85	♦ AKQJ1062
♣ A4	♣ KQ	♣ AK5

(a) This is a classic 2♠ opener.

(b) Open 2♥, planning to bid diamonds next time (you know you'll get a rebid, because your partner is forced to respond).

(c) Open 2♦. Even though you are a point short, your massive playing strength (nine tricks in your own hand) more than compensate for the lack of a twentieth point.

must know
The negative response to 2♦/♥/♠ is 2NT. This shows you have (only) up to seven points in your hand. Compare this to the negative response to the convention 2♣, which is 2♦ (see p. 159).

Responding to 2♦, 2♥, 2♠

Responder must bid something – all Two-of-a-suit openers are forcing for at least one round (for good reason: opener knows there's a very good chance of game or more and doesn't want his partner simply to pass). Indeed opener is bound to have slam in mind and responder's first duty is to tell opener whether slam is possible. For this purpose, responder has a special 'negative' bid, which is 2NT (meaning: 'Sorry, but there's no slam'). Following this bid, opener will bid again, but she'll now know that the deal belongs either in part-score or, more likely, in game.

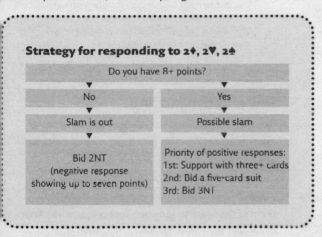

Strategy for responding to 2♦, 2♥, 2♠

Do you have 8+ points?

No	Yes
Slam is out	Possible slam
Bid 2NT (negative response showing up to seven points)	Priority of positive responses: 1st: Support with three+ cards 2nd: Bid a five-card suit 3rd: Bid 3NT

Let's consider your response to your partner's opening 2♠ with each of the following hands:

(a)
♠ 4
♥ 87532
♦ 9873
♣ J84

(b)
♠ Q72
♥ A973
♦ QJ5
♣ 983

(c)
♠ 8752
♥ Q9
♦ QJ62
♣ 975

(a) 2NT, the 'negative' response. You may be tempted not to respond at all. It's true that a spade game is unlikely, but if your partner has a second suit in hearts or diamonds (and she could easily be five-five) then passing may result in her going down in 2♠ with a game in a red suit available. Plus it's not good for partnership morale – your partner has made a forcing bid.

(b) 3♠ (or 4♠). By not responding 2NT you are showing a 'positive' hand, and therefore some slam interest.

(c) You know that the partnership should rest in 4♠. The trouble with bidding it immediately is that your partner will read you for a positive hand, and may advance to slam. Start with the negative 2NT, then jump to 4♠. That way, your partner will know to leave the bidding right there.

Pre-emptive bidding

A pre-empt is a bid that consumes large amounts of 'bidding space'. Typically your hand will be weak and you won't expect to make the number of tricks implied by your bid. You bid a pre-empt primarily to make life awkward for your opponents. By robbing them of the space to communicate properly, you hope to prevent them from landing in their best spot, either by shutting them up, pushing them too high or jostling them into the wrong trump suit. Losing a few points above the line on your score-pad (see pp. 220–1) is far better than allowing your opponents to make a game – or even a slam. But a word of warning: if you're vulnerable (have one game towards a rubber), your hand should have decent playing strength in it in order to pre-empt, as doubled vulnerable undertricks are quite expensive (see p. 224).

must know
- Strong hands open at the Two level; weak, pre-emptive hands open at the Three (or Four) level.
- After pre-empting, don't bid again.

When you pre-empt, you must decide how high you are prepared to bid, bid it, then don't bid again.

Opening at the Three level

This is the classic pre-empt. The Three-Level opening bid shows:

- A good seven-card suit (headed by two of the top three honours, or three of the top five honours).
- Less than opening points (3–10).

Consider whether you should open pre-emptively with the following hands:

(a)	(b)	(c)	(d)
♠ KQJ10532	♠ 75	♠ 4	♠ 9865
♥ 5	♥ 8	♥ A876532	♥ 8
♦ 863	♦ QJ109532	♦ 76	♦ 4
♣ 86	♣ KQ2	♣ J106	♣ KJ108753

(a) Yes, this is a textbook 3♠ opener: a very good suit (six almost certain tricks) and nothing else. The less you have outside your suit, the more confident you can be that your opponents will make a contract (typically a game), rendering your attempt to prevent them all the more worthwhile.

(b) Yes, open 3♦. Again you'd expect to make six tricks facing nothing (five diamonds – all bar ♦AK – plus a club).

(c) No. The suit is too bare. Pass.

(d) Yes, open 3♣.

Responding to Three-level openers

A Three-level opener aims to muck things up for the opponents. It also says to your partner, 'I've a poor hand in high cards, and I'm only interested in one trump suit. Please don't bid too much, and please don't try a suit of your own (or no-trumps) as that will render my hand useless'.

Responder's strategy can be summed up as: 'Put up or shut up!' The figure below outlines the twin strategies for responding to a Three-level opener: bidding to spoil and bidding to make.

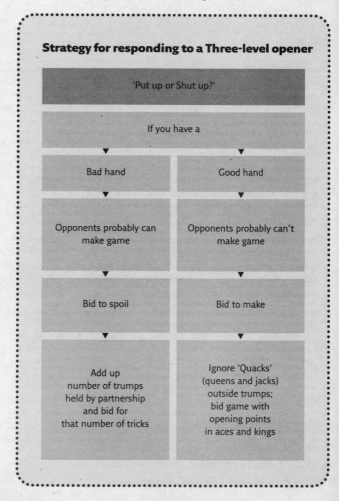

Strategy for responding to a Three-level opener

'Put up or Shut up?'

If you have a

Bad hand	Good hand
Opponents probably can make game	Opponents probably can't make game
Bid to spoil	Bid to make
Add up number of trumps held by partnership and bid for that number of tricks	Ignore 'Quacks' (queens and jacks) outside trumps; bid game with opening points in aces and kings

Let's now look at some responses to Three-level openers.

If your partner opens 3♠, and the next hand passes, the only two bids you should consider are pass and 4♠. Which option would you take with the following hands?

(a)	(b)	(c)	(d)
♠ A	♠ 5	♠ 87	♠ 987
♥ KJ8732	♥ AK74	♥ KQJ4	♥ 102
♦ AK5	♦ A742	♦ KQJ4	♦ A2
♣ KQ2	♣ A942	♣ QJ4	♣ J95432

Imagine that your hand is facing hand (a) on p. 151 (a typical pre-empt). I shall refer to this as hand (x).

(a) Bid 4♠ (not 4♥). Your ♠A is probably better than your partner's hearts and his spades are far better than your broken hearts. Pairing (a) with (x), you can see that 4♠ would make, in comfort, seven trump tricks, ♦AK and an easily establishable force winner in clubs. In 4♥, on the other hand, you'd flounder; your partner's hand would be useless in this instance.

(b) Bid 4♠. You have four tricks for your partner, and you'd expect six tricks from him. Put (b) facing (x) and you see that his six trump tricks plus your four side-suit tops make 4♠. Note that you don't need any real support for his suit, because he's promised a self-supporting suit; even a void can suffice as 'support'. The one bid you mustn't make is 3NT as you'd lose your means of getting back to your partner's spades after dislodging the opponents' ace.

(c) You have the same point count as hand (b), but put your hand opposite hand (x) and you see how much less useful your hand is. In fact you won't even make 3♠ – without aces and ♣K. Your partner needs quick tricks facing his short side-suits: aces and to a lesser extent kings. Queens and jacks ('quacks') are pretty useless (see the strategy for responding to a Three-level opener on p. 152). You should pass.

(d) Your hand is so poor that where your partner probably thinks the opponents have a high contract available, you certainly know they do. Pair your hand up with (x) and consider what they could make with their 26 cards. They are certain to make 12 tricks (a small slam) in hearts. You must stop them! Following the principle we met when supporting overcalls, if you want to spoil things for the opponents then bid to the 'level of the fit', i.e. work out how many cards are held by your side, and bid for that number of tricks. With ten spades, the correct bid is 4♠ – not expecting to make this, but hoping to create difficulties for the opponent who hasn't yet spoken. This opponent is certain to have a good hand with lots of hearts but may not chance 5♥ facing a partner who has said nothing.

Opening at the Four level

These bids are also pre-emptive, but because you are bidding for one more trick, you should have one more card in the suit (i.e. eight). These eight cards must be reasonable as ten tricks is a lot to make. Although you're not expecting to reach that target, you need to finish close to it or the resulting penalty will sting!

Here are some examples of opening bids at the Four level:

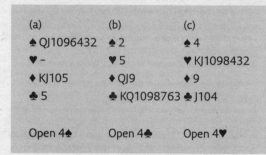

(a)	(b)	(c)
♠ QJ1096432	♠ 2	♠ 4
♥ –	♥ 5	♥ KJ1098432
♦ KJ105	♦ QJ9	♦ 9
♣ 5	♣ KQ1098763	♣ J104
Open 4♠	Open 4♣	Open 4♥

Repeating my earlier warning, if you're vulnerable, err on the side of caution. If vulnerable, hand (c) should arguably open 3♥, as 4♥ doubled could be expensive if your partner has no trick for you.

Pre-empting after opponent's opener

When your opponents have opened the bidding, you can still pre-empt, but you must 'double jump' (i.e. miss out two lower levels of your bid) in order to show a weak hand. (Although rarely used, a single jump overcall such as 1♥-3♣ is a strong bid.)

For example, if you were about to open 3♦, but your opponent opens before you and bids 1♣, you can still bid your intended 3♦ as it's a double jump (missing out 1♦ and 2♦ on the bidding ladder).

owever, if the opening bid was 1♥ or 1♠, the double-
imp bid would have to be 4♦, and that would only be
ound if you were planning to open 4♦ (i.e. you held
n eight-card suit). With 'only' seven diamonds, in
his case you could not pre-empt and, unless you had
nough overall strength (eight points or so) for a Two-
vel overcall, you would have to pass.

Now let's consider what you should bid after your
your right-hand opponent has opened 1♥:

(a)	(b)	(c)
♠ KQJ10532	♠ 75	♠ Q106
♥ 65	♥ 8	♥ 8
♦ 108	♦ QJ95432	♦ 4
♣ 86	♣ QJ8	♣ KQ987532

(a) Bid 3♠ – the bid you were planning to open
with. 3♠ is a double-jump overcall.

(b) Pass. To make the double-jump, you'd have to
bid 4♦, and that would be somewhere between
cavalier and suicidal, lacking the eighth diamond
(among other things).

(c) Bid 4♣ – the bid you were planning to open
with. This is acceptable because you have a good
eight-card suit.

Vhat to do if your opponents pre-empt

's not easy! The pre-emptor has taken away much
f your bidding space – that was her point. But don't
e frightened of bidding – remember that one of the
pposing hands is weak with little defence.

Here's a simple guideline. When your opponent
pens 3♥, pretend that she has opened 1♥ and
onsider the following:

if you would have overcalled 1NT (15–19 points with
heart stopper), then try a 3NT overcall.

if you would have made a take-out double of 1♥

> **must know**
> • You can pre-empt
> after an opponent opens
> the bidding, but only by
> making a double jump
> (i.e. missing out two
> lower bids of your suit).
> • Don't pre-empt after
> your partner has
> opened.
> • Be more wary
> pre-empting when you
> are vulnerable.

(showing an opening hand, short in hearts, with the other three suits well held), then try doubling 3♥ – also for take-out (as your partner has not yet bid).

• if you would have made a suit overcall of 1♠ over your opponent's 1♥, then check your hand is strong enough to make an overcall of, say 3♠, as it would need to be stronger at this level: around opening points (or more) and a very good suit of five (more likely six) cards.

Here are some examples. Your right-hand opponent has opened 3♥. What should you bid with each of the following hands?

(a)	(b)	(c)	(d)
♠ J7	♠ AQ62	♠ KQ1098	♠ 53
♥ AQ	♥ 3	♥ 53	♥ KJ109
♦ KQ1074	♦ KJ8	♦ AK42	♦ AQ4
♣ AJ53	♣ A8743	♣ 87	♣ A532

(a) Bid 3NT. The textbook point guide for a 3NT overcall is 16+. You don't have to be strictly balanced (a long suit to set up would be nice), but must hold a stopper in the opponent's suit. Here you have two stoppers, as ♥K is sure to be sitting on your right.

(b) Double. An opening hand, short in hearts, with three+ cards in all other suits: perfect for a double of a 1♥ opener, and perfect for a double of a 3♥ opener.

(c) Overcall 3♠, though it's arguable – your partner may easily raise you to a failing 4♠. But you simply can't afford to be talked out of the bidding. In the old days, 'It's too dangerous to bid' was often said. These days, you're more likely to hear: 'It's too dangerous to pass' (though, admittedly, often as an attempt to justify an overly ambitious bid).

(d) Pass. You'd like to double 3♥ for penalties, but this would be for take-out (your partner having not bid). So keep quiet, and enjoy the defence (assuming your partner also passes). If your partner reopens with a take-out double, you should again pass – even though your partner is asking you to choose another suit. He'll be surprised, but you have effectively converted the take-out double into a penalty double in order to defend a heart contract. Your partner will cheer up as your defence to a doubled 3♥ progresses, and the tricks come rolling in.

---

ow let's consider what happens when your left-hand
pponent opens at the three level and your partner
oubles (for take-out). On p. 128, we learnt that you
vould jump the bidding with nine+ points when
sponding to a take-out double. The logic of this is
at, forced to bid, a bid at the lowest level is consistent
ith nothing. But when you have something (i.e. nine+
oints) you must show it. Exactly the same principle
pplies to pre-emptive situations.

Bearing in mind what has just been said, look at
the following examples and consider what you
should bid in each case. The bidding so far is 3♥-
double-pass (your left-hand opponent opened 3♥,
your partner doubled, and your right-hand-
opponent passed).

(a)   (b)
♠ 10532   ♠ KQ1075
♥ A765   ♥ 98
♦ 1084   ♦ KJ32
♣ 76   ♣ 98

(a) Bid 3♠.

(b) Bid 4♣. Here you have nine points and so
should jump the bidding up a level.

Useful tip

If your opponent opens the bidding at the Three level, consider what you
would have done had she opened at the One level. If you would have
doubled a One-level opener with your current hand, then double a Three-
level opener (both for take-out); if you would have overcalled 1NT over a
One-level opener, then consider a 3NT overcall over a Three-level opener.

The Opening 2♣ convention

Opening 2♣ is the strongest of all opening bids, completely unrelated to clubs and, as such, a universally played convention. It shows your very strong hand and asks your partner to keep open the bidding until game is reached.

must know
Although high-card points do not tell the full story (see pp. 190–5), a 2♣ opener will normally contain 23 or more points. 2♦, 2♥, 2♠ openers will normally contain slightly fewer: 20–22 points.

When to use 2♣

By opening 2♣, you are showing any hand with the very high point score of 23 or more. However, if you think you can make game facing virtually nothing in your partner's hand, then you can open 2♣ with a little fewer than 23 points. The bid says in effect: 'This deal belongs to our side in game or slam'.

Here are some examples of 2♣ openers:

(a)	(b)	(c)
♠ AQ1084	♠ 2	♠ AQJ
♥ AKQ2	♥ AKQJ52	♥ AJ2
♦ AQ7	♦ AQJ9	♦ AQJ9
♣ K	♣ A2	♣ KJ9

Note that hand (b) may be a couple of high-card points short, but in fact (b) is much the strongest hand of the three: even if your partner has no points at all, a 4♥ game will be made whenever ♦9 wins the fourth round of diamonds.

Responding to 2♣

The negative 'I think slam is unlikely' response is 2♦, on the grounds of economy. Over that response, a 2NT rebid by opener shows 23–24 points and a balanced hand. Responder can then pass if he's got absolutely nothing, but this is the only time responder can pass a 2♣ opener in the run up to game.

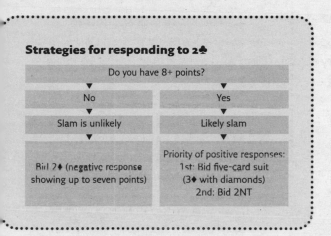

Strategies for responding to 2♣

Do you have 8+ points?	
▼	▼
No	Yes
▼	▼
Slam is unlikely	Likely slam
▼	
Bid 2♦ (negative response showing up to seven points)	Priority of positive responses: 1st: Bid five-card suit (3♦ with diamonds) 2nd: Bid 2NT

Let's consider what your response should be with each of the following hands after your partner has opened 2♣:

(a)	(b)	(c)
♠ 754	♠ J	♠ Q1062
♥ 742	♥ J98542	♥ A2
♦ 87	♦ Q2	♦ KJ963
♣ 76432	♣ Q972	♣ 92

(a) You may feel like passing, but don't! Your partner may have a void club and/or a game in her hand. The correct negative response is 2♦.

(b) Respond 2♦. You have a fine heart suit, but to bid 2♥ would show a positive hand (i.e. eight+ points), and might lead your partner into a failing slam contract. The correct strategy is to make the negative response, then bid hearts.

(c) Show a positive hand with diamonds, but bid 3♦ not 2♦, because 2♦ is the conventional negative response to a 2♣ opener, and unrelated to diamonds (see the strategy table above).

must know

If your partner opens 2♣, you must always respond, taking him to the level of game – unless he rebids 2NT (showing a 23-24 point balanced hand), in which case you can pass, if holding nothing.

must know

A hand with 23 points or
more should be opened
2♣. If you have less than
23 points, only open 2♣
if you think you can
make game on the
strength of your hand
alone – with little help
from partner.

Now, by way of a refresher of other Two-level openers
(pages 120–4), compare the bidding strategies for
the following pairs of hands (South is dealer):

(a)	(b)	(c)
North	North	North
♠ QJ9642	♠ A532	♠ 976
♥ 3	♥ 108	♥ 86
♦ J1084	♦ 76	♦ AK874
♣ 65	♣ 97432	♣ J62
South	South	South
♠ K10	♠ 7	♠ AKQ103
♥ K842	♥ AKQ952	♥ KQ
♦ AK92	♦ AQ9	♦ J3
♣ AK4	♣ AJ6	♣ AKQ5

The bidding:

(a)		(b)		(c)	
South	North	South	North	South	North
2NT (i)	4♠ (ii)	2♥ (i)	2NT (ii)	2♣ (i)	3♦ (ii)
Pass (iii)		3♥ (iii)	4♥ (iv)	3♠ (iii)	4♠ (iv)
		Pass		4NT (v)	5♦ (vi)
				6♠ (vii)	Pass

(a)

(i) Bid shows 20–22 points and a balanced hand.
(ii) Bid shows a six-card spade suit (facing at least
two spades), and (within one point) the points for
game.
(iii) Having opened 2NT and described his hand,
South gives over control of the auction to North.

(b)

(i) Bid shows a good five/six card suit, 20–22 points
and an unbalanced hand. It is forcing for one round.
(ii) Negative response, showing fewer than eight
points.
(iii) Bid shows a sixth heart with nothing else to
offer. If North is without suitable cards, South is
offering a way out.
(iv) Bid shows a fit for hearts (facing six cards).
North's hand is well worth the raise: one ace (and
possible trumping potential in diamonds) is
ample (one ace is better than two queens, and
much better than four jacks).

(c)

(i) Bid shows 23+ points, any shape. (Opening 2♣ convention.)

(ii) Positive hand (8+ points). North shows his decent five-card diamond suit.

(iii) The auction is probably heading for slam, but there's no rush. South shows his five-card spade suit (with four he would be balanced, and rebid no-trumps). He awaits developments.

(iv) Bid shows three-card support, and no substantial extra values.

(v) Bid asks: 'How many aces do you have?' (Blackwood convention)

(vi) Response: 'One'

(vii) Bid says: 'Oh good. There's just one missing ace – I expect it to be our only loser'.

The play:

Here's how to play out the recommended contracts:

Contract of 4♠ by North (ten tricks to make):

```
                North (Declarer)
                ♠ QJ9642
West            ♥ 3              East
♠ A8            ♦ J1084          ♠ 753
♥ Q1065         ♣ 65             ♥ AJ97
♦ Q763                           ♦ 5
♣ Q97                            ♣ J10832
                South (Dummy)
                ♠ K10
                ♥ K842
                ♦ AK92
                ♣ AK4
```

East leads ♦5, a very dangerous start to the defence. You (declarer – North), looking at the combined diamond length, suspect a singleton lead. You win dummy's ♦K and (as there's no reason to delay drawing trumps) lead ♠K (highest from the shorter length). West wins ♠A (correctly interpreting the opening lead) returns a second diamond. East trumps and switches safely to ♣J. You win dummy's ♣K, then lead ♠10, overtaking with ♠J (drawing the two remaining missing trumps). A trick short, you now lead ♥3, in an effort to promote ♥K. East may play low, but say he rises with ♥A, you can win his

must know

There is no "weakness take-out" after partner opens Two Notrumps. If you don't pass, you'll end up in game.

must know

- A negative conventional response of 2♦ to a 2♣ opener means that responder holds less than eight points and is warning the opener not to go for slam.

- After a positive response to a 2♣ opener, bidding proceeds with the partnership trying to find a fit, and possibly go for slam.

club return with ♣A, and cash the promoted ♥K, discarding a diamond loser. Ten tricks and game made.

Contract of 4♥ by South (ten tricks to make):

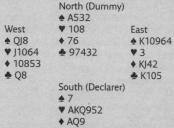

```
              North (Dummy)
              ♠ A532
West          ♥ 108          East
♠ QJ8         ♦ 76           ♠ K10964
♥ J1064       ♣ 97432        ♥ 3
♦ 10853                      ♦ KJ42
♣ Q8                         ♣ K105
              South (Declarer)
              ♠ 7
              ♥ AKQ952
              ♦ AQ9
              ♣ AJ6
```

West leads ♠Q, showing ♠J and denying ♠K. You (declarer – South) win dummy's ♠A, noting that dummy has fewer diamonds than you (telling you to delay drawing trumps). At Trick two, you lead ♦6 to ♦2, and ♦Q. Your finesse successful, cash ♦A, voiding dummy of diamonds, then trump ♦9 in dummy (giving you an extra trick). Then lead dummy's remaining trump to your ♥AKQ. East discards on the second round – to reveal an unlucky four-one split. However, this only costs you the overtrick (extra trick above the number contracted), as all you lose are two clubs and a trump. Ten tricks and game made.

Contract of 6♠ by South (12 tricks to make):

```
              North (Dummy)
              ♠ 976
West          ♥ 86           East
♠ 4           ♦ AK874        ♠ J852
♥ A9753       ♣ J62          ♥ J1042
♦ 10652                      ♦ Q9
♣ 1098                       ♣ 743
              South (Declarer)
              ♠ AKQ103
              ♥ KQ
              ♦ J3
              ♣ AKQ5
```

Against a slam, the goal for the defence is merely two tricks, so it's usually best for the opening leader to cash an ace (if he has one), even if it is unsupported by the king, as in this case. Note that this would be very unwise against a lower-level contract (a 'hare move'). So West leads ♥A, hoping his partner has ♥K or a singleton, or perhaps a 'slow trick' (one that makes much later) elsewhere. At Trick two, West continues with a second heart (he may switch to ♣10 – but it doesn't matter to you), and you (declarer – South) win in hand, then cash ♠AK. West then discards, revealing the four-one trump split, but as it's West and not East who discards you are able to finesse the ♠J held by East. You cross to dummy's ♦K, then lead a third trump to East's ♠8 and your ♠10. You cash ♠Q, felling East's ♠J, and claim the remainder in top tricks: 12 tricks and slam made.

Useful tip

Opening hands with 20–22 points and very good clubs present a problem. Unable to open 2♣ to mean clubs, you are best opening 1♣ and hoping your partner can respond.

The Stayman convention

Invented simultaneously both sides of the Atlantic around the time of World War Two, then popularized by New Yorker Sam Stayman, this convention is one of the three most popular conventions (with Blackwood and the 2♣ opener).

must know

The Stayman convention is the only way to locate a four-four fit in a major suit when responding to a 1NT opener. This is important because, if a fit exists, and the values for game are present, then declaring Four-of-that-major gives you a higher chance of winning than any other game contract.

Why use Stayman?

The top priority in the bidding is to locate an eight-card fit in a major suit. Should one exist, together with the values for game, then it's almost certainly winning bridge to declare Four-of-that-major (4♥ or 4♠).

Study the following responses to 1NT (see also pp. 59–63):

(a)	(b)	(c)
♠ KJ8643	♠ AQ762	♠ KQ43
♥ 7	♥ 74	♥ 98
♦ A10	♦ AQ32	♦ AJ92
♣ KJ85	♣ Q2	♣ QJ4

(a) Bid 4♠. There's a known eight-card spade fit (your partner must have at least two spades for his 1NT), plus the values for game (the powerful shape more than compensates for the possible lack of a 25th point). The six-two major fit is easy to reach.

(b) Bid 3♠. You don't have a definite eight-card spade fit, because your partner may have only two spades. Jumping to 3♠ shows a game-forcing hand with precisely five spades, enabling opener to bid 3NT with a doubleton spade, or 4♠ with three or more spades. In this way you'll locate a five-three major fit.

(c) You might simply jump to 3NT, but if your partner holds four cards in spades, you're almost certainly better off in 4♠ (look at those weak hearts). Here's where the Stayman convention is needed: to help you locate a four-four major fit.

164 | Beginner's Guide to Bridge

How Stayman works

The Stayman convention sacrifices the 2♣ response to 1NT, previously used as a weakness take-out into clubs, for a 2♣ bid that asks the question:

> 'Partner, do you have a four-card major in your 1NT opener?'

In reply, the 1NT opener bids a major if he holds a four-card major (hearts with four cards in both majors), and otherwise he replies 2♦. This is summarized below.

Stayman: the mechanics

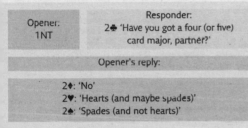

Opener: 1NT	Responder: 2♣ 'Have you got a four (or five) card major, partner?'
Opener's reply:	
2♦: 'No' 2♥: 'Hearts (and maybe spades)' 2♠: 'Spades (and not hearts)'	

The only other situation when Stayman is used is after a 2NT opener (or 2♣ 2♦-2NT). In this case, a 3♣ response asks the 2NT bidder for a four-card major. His replies are identical to those given for the 2♣ response, but one level higher.

When to use Stayman

Clearly the responder to 1NT must have a four-card major – the reason for applying the convention is to locate a four-four major suit fit. Normally he will have at least game-invitational values (i.e. eleven+ points), and his hand won't be too flat (something like 4333). Otherwise, he should simply raise no-trumps and not bother with major-suit fit-finding.

must know
Responder can bid Stayman with fewer than eleven points when he can cater to all opener's replies. Usually this means he will have five-four in the majors (five cards in one and four in the other).

Look again at hand (c) on p. 164. Here you have a perfect hand for Stayman – the only way a 4-4 spade fit can be located. If your partner replies 2♠ to your 2♣, you should jump to 4♠ as you now know there's a spade fit plus the values for game. If the reply is 2♦ or 2♥, you should jump to 3NT instead.

Let's consider whether each of the following hands should bid 2♣ (Stayman) in response to your partner's 1NT opener:

(a)	(b)	(c)	(d)	(e)
♠ 74	♠ Q72	♠ KJ743	♠ KJ743	♠ QJ42
♥ J862	♥ J974	♥ Q84	♥ Q984	♥ J10854
♦ A1052	♦ AQ2	♦ A2	♦ A	♦ 7
♣ AQ3	♣ KJ9	♣ QJ4	♣ QJ4	♣ 973

(a) Yes, bid 2♣ (Stayman). You have game-invitational values and want to search for a four-four heart fit because no-trumps looks dangerous with your spade weakness. If your partner replies 2♥, you should invite game by bidding 3♥ (asking 'Are you minimum or maximum, partner?'). If your partner replies 2♦ or 2♠, bid 2NT. This shows the same strength of hand as 1NT–2NT (i.e. 11–12 points) and, thus, invites game in no-trumps. Take away a point from your hand and you should pass 1NT (as should any 0–10 point hand without a five-card suit). The problem with bidding Stayman now is that you have no follow-up should your partner reply 2♦ or 2♠ (2NT would show an interest in game).

(b) No, don't bid 2♣. Your hand is so flat it's hard to see how 4♥ (even if your partner has four cards in hearts) will play much better than what you should bid, which is 3NT.

(c) No, don't bid 2♣. You have no four-card major. To locate a five-three major-fit, jump to 3♠.

(d) Yes, bid 2♣, not because of your five spades (a fit there can be found via a jump to 3♠), but because of your four hearts. If your partner replies 2♥ or 2♠, jump to game in that major; if she replies 2♦, make the bid you would have made before you played Stayman, i.e. 3♠. As with the direct response of 3♠ to 1NT, this asks your partner to raise to 4♠ if she has three spades, or otherwise to bid 3NT. Thus by bidding 2♣, then 3♠ over a 2♦ reply, you have managed to check whether an eight-card fit in either major exists (a four-four heart fit or a five-three/five-four spade fit).

(e) Yes, bid 2♣. Usually responder should have at least game-invitational values to bid Stayman so he can cater to all opener's replies. Here's an exception: when you have five-four in the majors, because you clearly can handle any reply in this case. You should pass 2♥ or 2♠, and convert 2♦ to 2♥ (meaning the same as 1NT-2♥, i.e. a weakness take-out). You'll be pleased to have bid Stayman rather than an immediate 2♥ if your partner has four or five spades, and just two hearts.

'Phoney Stayman'

We learnt on p. 36 the usefulness of a weakness take-out in removing your partner's 1NT opener to Two-of-a-suit. A problem occurs when Stayman prevents you from doing this in clubs because the weakness take-out bid into clubs and Stayman are the same: 2♣. However, there is a way you can still use 2♣ as a weakness take-out into clubs. Say you have a weak hand in response to 1NT, with six clubs, and are desperate to make clubs trumps. Bid 2♣ and follow it (over your partner's reply) with 3♣. This, in effect, says: 'Partner, cancel the Stayman message. All I want to do is get out in clubs. Because of the convention we now have to play 3♣. You must now pass.' (Note that you don't jump to 3♣ immediately – that remains a rare bid, reserved for very shapely and, usually, slam-interested hands with long clubs.)

Here is a summary of when a responder to a 1NT opener should use Stayman (2♣):

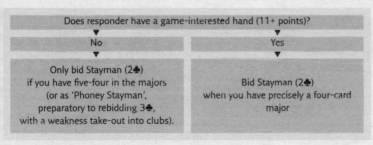

Does responder have a game-interested hand (11+ points)?	
▼	▼
No	Yes
▼	▼
Only bid Stayman (2♣) if you have five-four in the majors (or as 'Phoney Stayman', preparatory to rebidding 3♣, with a weakness take-out into clubs).	Bid Stayman (2♣) when you have precisely a four-card major

Opener's continuations

For his immediate reply to the Stayman 2♣, opener should bid either 2♦, 2♥ or 2♠, as appropriate (no other bid is acceptable). When responder makes his next bid, opener should simply strip away the 'Stayman part' of the auction to determine the overall meaning. Thus the sequence 1NT-2♣-2♦-2♥, like 1NT-2♥, shows 0–10 points with five hearts, and is a weakness take-out; 1NT-2♣-2♦-3♥, like 1NT-3♥, shows a game-force with precisely five hearts. (On both occasions, presumably responder bid Stayman because he also has four spades.)

How about 1NT-2♣-2♥-3NT? Is opener always expected to pass, as in 1NT-3NT? The answer is no. In this case, responder presumably has four spades – he must have four of one major to bid Stayman, and he seems nonplussed with hearts. So if opener began 1NT, with four spades as well as four hearts, his next bid should be to remove 3NT to 4♠.

Let's consider how the following pairs of hands should be bid.

	(a)		(b)	
	North		North	
	♠ AQ42		♠ AQ32	
	♥ 42		♥ AK732	
	♦ AK75		♦ 4	
	♣ 532		♣ AK2	
	South		South	
	♠ KJ109		♠ KJ4	
	♥ AK76		♥ J65	
	♦ J6		♦ AK53	
	♣ J87		♣ 1087	

Bidding:

South	North	South	North
1NT (i)	2♣ (ii)	1NT (i)	2♣ (ii)
2♥ (iii)	3NT (iv)	2♦ (iii)	3♥ (iv)
4♠ (v)	Pass	4♥ (v)	6♥(vi)
		Pass	

(a)

The bidding:

(i) Opener bids 1NT showing a balanced hand with 12–14 points.

(ii) Responder (North) bids Stayman (a request for four-card majors). North is almost sure (looking at his weak hearts and clubs) that a 4♠ game (should your partner hold four spades) will play better than 3NT.

(iii) Opener bids hearts, showing four (five) cards in both majors.

(iv) Responder assumes that opener doesn't have four spades, so reverts to 3NT.

(v) Opener knows that responder must have four spades (why else did he bother with Stayman?). So he corrects to 4♠.

The play:
In a 3NT game, the declarer starts with only eight tricks (even if the opponents don't cash five or six club tricks), whereas in 4♠, though he starts with eight tricks, he can make two extra tricks in the trump suit. He does this by delaying drawing trumps and playing ♥AK (voiding dummy), then trumping ♥6 (with ♠Q), back to ♠9, and trumping ♥7 (with ♠A). He can then draw trumps and cash ♦AK for ten tricks.

(b)
The bidding:
(i) Opener bids 1NT showing a balanced hand with 12–14 points.
(ii) Responder uses Stayman to find a four-four spade fit. The hearts are irrelevant, because a heart fit can be found by jumping to 3♥ (as we see in the next few steps).
(iii) Opener's reply means: no four-card major.
(iv) Responder knows there's no spade fit, but there may still be a five-three heart fit. His 3♥, like 1NT-3♥, shows a game-forcing hand with precisely five hearts.
(v) Opener raises to 4♥ with three-card support.
(vi) Responder knows there are a minimum of 32 partnership points and a fit. His 5431 shape is arguably the most powerful among the common shapes. There's no point in using Blackwood, as he has no concern about aces (holding all but one).

The play:
Provided the declarer (North) can draw trumps for the loss of at most one trick, he will make his small slam via four spade tricks, four trumps and the minor-suit ace-kings. To maximize his chances of losing just one trump, he should win, say, an opening diamond lead with the king (in dummy), then cross to ♥A (or ♥K), then lead a low heart towards ♥J. Trying to promote dummy's ♥J via a finesse (leading from the opposite hand) will be necessary if the second hand (i.e. East) holds ♥Q1098 (see the diagram below).

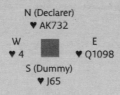

```
            N (Declarer)
              ♥ AK732
   W                        E
   ♥ 4                      ♥ Q1098
            S (Dummy)
              ♥ J65
```

Wrong: Lead ♥J. Declarer will lose two tricks.
Wrong: Cash ♥A and ♥K. Declarer will lose two tricks.
Right: Cash ♥A (or ♥K), then lead towards ♥J. If East plays low (or ♥Q), ♥J is promoted. Declarer will lose just one trick.
NB: If both opponents follow to the second heart, declarer doesn't mind losing to ♥Q, as ♥K will fell the last heart.

Bidding review

It's time to make sure you've mastered the key principles that opener and responder should adhere to, and the stage that follows (i.e. second bids, 'rebids'). Then we'll go a step further to look at strategies for dealing with opponents who intervene.

Opening the bidding

• **Whether to open:** Always open with 12+ points. Open with less when you satisfy the Rule of 20 (where total high-card points plus number of cards in the two longest suits reach 20).

• **Balanced or unbalanced:** Your whole bidding strategy depends on whether your hand is balanced (4432, 4333, 5332). With a balanced hand, you should open, or plan to rebid, no-trumps.

• **Which suit to open:** Always open the longest suit, and choose the higher-ranking of equally long suits (with one exception: open 1♥ with four-four in the majors).

What would you open with the following hands?

(a)	(b)	(c)
♠ 8	♠ AQ72	♠ KJ743
♥ KQ972	♥ Q974	♥ Q98
♦ A10532	♦ AKJ	♦ A32
♣ J5	♣ 32	♣ QJ

(a) Open 1♥ – using the Rule of 20 (see p. 54), and choosing the higher-ranking suit.

(b) Open 1♥ – the exception. Plan to rebid in no-trumps unless your partner responds 1♠, thereby revealing an eight-card major-suit fit (a top priority). Note the reason for the exception: starting with 1♥, you make it much easier to find a fit in the other major (opening 1♠ may result in a heart fit being missed).

(c) Open 1NT (not 1♠). With a balanced hand and 12–14 points, you must open 1NT. The great advantage of opening 1NT is that you don't need to find a rebid over a change of suit from responder (you can pass).

Responding to One-of-a-suit

- **Whether to respond:** Pass with less then six points. Respond with six or more.
- **Support for opener's suit:** With four-card support, use the Responder's Support Line as a guide (see p. 65). Be prepared to upgrade your strategy with side-suit shortages.
- **No support:** If you can't support your partner's opening suit, bid your longest suit at the lowest level, choosing the cheaper of four-card suits and the higher-ranking of five-card suits. You won't be able to bid a new suit at the Two level, however, unless you can satisfy the Rule of 14 (total high-card points + number of cards in that suit must reach 14). Instead, you'll probably have to bid the 'dustbin 1NT' (see p. 68).
- **New suit responses:** Typically, these only guarantee four cards in the bid suit. However a new major response at the Two Level (1♠-2♥ being the only example), unless the opponents intervene, guarantees *five* cards.

must know
- Ranking of suits: clubs rank lowest, then diamonds, then hearts and finally spades, the highest ranked suit.
- Ranking of bids: a bid must always be higher than the previous bid. A bid is higher if it is a larger number or the same number but in a higher ranking denomination. The ranking order is: no trumps (the highest), spades, hearts, diamonds and clubs (the lowest) – see p. 22. For example, a bid of 1♥ may be followed by 1♠ or 2♣, but not 1♣.
- High-card points: to estimate the strength of your hand, count points as follows: ace = 4, king = 3, queen = 2, jack = 1

When responding:

- Don't jump a level when you are bidding a new suit.
- A single major raise with just three-card support usually works better than if you respond 1NT.
- New suit responses only guarantee four(+) cards, except for new majors at the Two level, which show a minimum of five cards.

In this example, your partner has opened 1♥. What would you respond with the following hands?

(a)	(b)	(c)
♠ 8	♠ Q72	♠ KJ43
♥ Q972	♥ 4	♥ 98
♦ AQ532	♦ Q107542	♦ A2
♣ K85	♣ K65	♣ AK632

(a) Respond 4♥. You have just eleven high-card points, but the singleton spade is worth about three more.

(b) Respond 1NT. You fail the Rule of 14, so should settle for the 'dustbin 1NT'. Note that over a 1♠ opener, the correct response would be 2♠. A single major raise does not guarantee four-card support, and supporting with three cards is usually preferable to the nebulous 1NT response.

(c) Repond 2♣, i.e. bid your longest suit at the lowest level. You'll make sure the bidding reaches (at least) game, but for now you're in the 'fit-finding stage' of the auction and shouldn't waste bidding space by jumping the bidding.

Opener's rebid

Now we turn to that most pivotal of bids, the opener's rebid. When opening One-of-a-suit, opener shows a wide array of hand-types: anything from 12 to 19 points (less if satisfying the Rule of 20), four or more cards in the suit opened, and either a balanced or an unbalanced hand. It's the opener's rebid that really pinpoints the strength and shape of his hand. The opener rebids after hearing support from his partner, or, alternatively, after hearing a change of suit.

After hearing support

Once opener knows he has support, the bidding is relatively straightforward. The trump suit has been found and it's now a question of determining which zone the partnership lies within: part-score, game or perhaps slam.

Let's look at some examples of rebids after your partner has indicated support. You've opened 1♠, and your partner has raised to 2♠ (showing 6–9 points):

(a)	(b)	(c)
♠ KJ643	♠ AJ862	♠ AKJ103
♥ 72	♥ KJ7	♥ Q8
♦ AKQ2	♦ A32	♦ AJ92
♣ AQ	♣ Q2	♣ Q2

(a) Rebid 4♠. You have enough points for game (19 in your hand + 6 minimum from your partner = 25).

(b) Pass. There's no chance of game. Even if responder has nine points, 25 partnership points can't be present as you have only 15 in your hand.

(c) Rebid 3♠. This invites the spade game and says, in effect: 'Partner, I know you have a bad hand. But do you have a bad, bad hand or a good, bad hand?' With nearer nine points, your partner (responder) will go on to bid 4♠; with nearer six, he'll pass. But note that responder should look at more than just his high-card points: he should also look at the quality (and length) of his trumps, and whether he has any trumping potential.

must know
A useful guide for when to go for game is if you and your partner together have 25 points (i.e. ten more than your opponents out of the total, 40). See 'bidding to a game contract' on pp. 31–4.

After hearing a change of suit

In this case, neither the trump suit nor the level have been resolved, but opener is now able to use his rebid to tell responder whether his hand is balanced. With a balanced hand, he'll indicate how many points he holds (to within a point or so); with an unbalanced hand, he'll further define the shape of his hand.

Opener's rebid strategy – according to shape

I hope you've come to realize the importance of the shape of a bridge hand. In this section we'll review the common shapes of an opening hand and go on to consider the opener's rebid strategy accordingly.

Describing hand shapes

	Unbalanced	Balanced
One-suiters	6322 6331	
	6421 6430	4432
Two-suiters	5431 5422 5521	4333
Three-suiters	4441	5332

Opener is balanced

In this case, opener shows his point count to within a narrow range by virtue of the number of no-trumps he rebids (see p. 55).

Opener is one-suited: 6322, 6331

Opener will want to stress the main feature of his hand, the six-card suit. By repeating the suit he strongly implies he has six cards. However, an opener's rebid of the same suit does more than merely show the six-card suit. It shows the strength of his hand according to the 'Opener's Six-card Repeat Line' below.

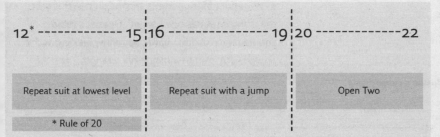

12^* ------------- 15 : 16 ------------- 19 : 20 ------------- 22

| Repeat suit at lowest level | Repeat suit with a jump | Open Two |

* Rule of 20

Opener's Six-card Repeat Line

Here are some examples of rebidding a one-suited hand. In each case you have opened 1♠ and your partner has responded 2♣:

(a)
♠ KJ8643
♥ 74
♦ AQ2
♣ J5

(b)
♠ AQJ962
♥ K4
♦ A32
♣ Q2

(c)
♠ AKJ43
♥ Q4
♦ J872
♣ J4

(a) Rebid 2♠. By opening and rebidding spades at the lowest level, you are showing six spades and up to 15 points.

(b) Rebid 3♠. By jumping a level in your suit, you are showing six spades and 16–19 points.

(c) Rebid 2♦. Don't repeat your spades – to do so would imply six cards. Your 2♦ rebid shows your five-four shape perfectly.

Opener is two-suited: 5431, 5422, 5521

With a two-suited hand, opener, in the hope of finding a fit with his partner's hand, has bid his first suit. When he doesn't find a fit with his first suit, he needs to rebid to try and a find a fit with his second suit. Sometimes there will be a happy scenario where responder actually replies in opener's second suit.

• Responder bids opener's second suit: In this case, the trump suit has been found. Opener's rebid should show his four-card support by bidding at the appropriate level to indicate his strength – see the 'Opener's Support Line' below.

Opener's Support Line

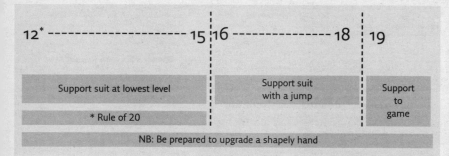

Let's look at some examples where your partner (responder) has bid your second suit in response to your opener. In each case you've opened 1♥ and your partner has responded 1♠. What should you rebid?

(a)	(b)	(c)
♠ J643	♠ AJ62	♠ AJ108
♥ AK874	♥ KJ984	♥ KQ432
♦ K82	♦ A2	♦ 2
♣ 5	♣ K2	♣ AK4

(a) Rebid 2♠. You have a minimum opener (Rule of 20), so you should support spades at the minimum level. Bear in mind that responder may only have six points and only four spades.

(b) Rebid 3♠. Your bid shows 16–18 points, or a little less to compensate for distribution. Responder is allowed to pass, but only needs a decent eight points before he'll try for 4♠ and game.

(c) Rebid 4♠. It would be feeble not to have a go at 4♠. If you add a nominal three points for the singleton diamond – about right when you have primary (four-card) support – you have 20 points.

• Responder doesn't bid opener's second suit: This is the more likely scenario – a fit still needs to be found. In this case, the opener's rebid must be his second suit. A universal bidding rule usefully applies here: by bidding a second suit, opener reveals that his first suit shows five+ cards, not merely four.

Because a fit hasn't been found, opener should avoid jumping the bidding, even with a good hand. His rebid should therefore be the second suit at the lowest level.

must know
Only in a case where opener has the guaranteed strength for game (i.e. 19 points) should he jump the bidding in a new suit. In all other cases, the opener's rebid of his second suit should be at the lowest level.

Here are some examples. In each of the following cases, you open 1♦ and your partner responds 1♠. What should your rebid be?

(a)	(b)	(c)
♠ 62	♠ K	♠ 108
♥ K4	♥ A4	♥ KQ42
♦ AK1082	♦ AK862	♦ AKJ63
♣ J932	♣ K9862	♣ 74

(a) Rebid 2♣. Your opener was a perfect 'five-four' (Rule of 20) bid. Note that bidding a new suit doesn't show any extra values. Don't worry, your partner won't leave you in clubs unless they are much better than his diamonds (he heard you bid diamonds first).

(b) Rebid 2♣. You have a good hand but it would be a mistake to waste 'bidding space' by jumping to 3♣. It would also (wrongly) indicate a game-going hand – your hand is not strong enough to insist on game. Your rebid simply shows your five-four shape; later you can hope to send news of your fifth club and above-minimum values.

(c) Rebid 2♥ but note this is contentious. A popular school of thought contends that to bid 2♥ (forcing responder to the Three level to give preference back to the first suit) is unwise. The 2♥ bid is termed a 'reverse'. My recommendation – at least at this stage – is to focus on showing your shape. Rebid 2♥ to show your five-four shape, and worry about getting a bit too high if and when this happens. (For the curious, the 'reversers' would rebid 2♦ with the hand shown. As you've probably worked out, they are unable to play one of the most attractive and helpful of rules: that repeating a suit shows six cards.)

Opener is both one-suited and two-suited: 6421, 6430

In this case, where opener has opened the six-card suit, and his partner responded in one of opener's two shorter suits, there's a choice of opener rebids. Opener can repeat his first suit, showing the six cards, but leaving the second suit unbid; or he can introduce the four-card suit, showing a five-four shape, but leaving the sixth card unbid. When there's a wild disparity of suit quality, e.g. the six-card suit is an excellent major and the four-card suit a poor minor, the first option is best: opener should ignore the four-card minor and repeat the six-card major. If the suits are roughly even in suit quality, then the simplest approach is to do what comes cheapest.

> Here's an example. You opened 1♥ with the hand shown below. What would you rebid over a response of (a) 1♠ and (b) 2♦?
>
> ♠ 52
> ♥ AQ8643
> ♦ 4
> ♣ AQ43
>
> (a) Rebid 2♣ – it's cheaper than 2♥.
> (b) Rebid 2♥ – it's cheaper than 3♣.

Opener is three-suited: 4441

Natural bidding is well-tailored to one-suited hands (bid and repeat – showing six cards); and two-suited hands (bid one, then bid the other – showing a five-four shape). But what about the dreaded three-suited shape of 4441? The only good thing to say about it is that it is relatively rare: mercifully less than 3 per cent of all hands.

There have been many theories about which suit to open (and what to rebid). Worthy of consideration among them is to pass with less than a good 14 points: perhaps an opponent will open your singleton suit, and you can double (for take-out); this would do in one bid what you would be unable, if you opened, to do in two.

Perhaps the best approach, however, both simple to remember and effective, is:

must know
The 'cheapest' bidding option is the bid that comes first as you work up the bidding hierarchy (on p. 22).

4 Development

With a black-suit singleton, open 1♥. With a red-suit singleton, open 1♣.

To remember, think 'Taps': 'C' for Clubs and 'H' for Hearts ('C' and 'H', Cold and Hot, are the two Taps).

What would you open with the following hands? Discuss your planned rebid if your partner responds in your singleton suit (likely).

(a)	(b)	(c)	(d)
♠ A964	♠ Q1072	♠ K864	♠ J
♥ KJ74	♥ 4	♥ KQJ4	♥ QJ94
♦ 2	♦ A982	♦ AJ72	♦ AQ102
♣ KQJ3	♣ AKJ4	♣ 3	♣ K742

(a) Open 1♣. Rebid 1♥ over the expected 1♦ response. Admittedly your partner will expect a fifth club, but, clubs being a minor-suit, this is a small lie.

(b) Open 1♣, and plan to rebid 1♠ over a 1♥ response.

(c) Open 1♥, and plan to rebid 2♦ over a 2♣ response. Lying about your fifth card in hearts, a major-suit, is a worry; with an extra point, you might consider a different lie: rebidding 2NT to show 15-16 'balanced'.

(d) Pass. A singleton spade is the most awkward 4441 and it is best to refrain from opening with less than a decent 14 points. With 14 points or more (make ♣7 into ♣Q for example), open 1♥ and choose between two slightly misdescriptive rebids over a 1♠ response: 1NT showing 15-16 'balanced' (you are a spade short), or 2♣ showing a five-four shape (you are a heart short).

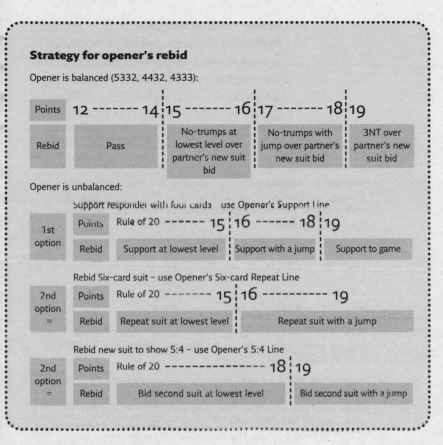

Strategy for opener's rebid

Opener is balanced (5332, 4432, 4333):

Points	12 ------- 14	15 ------- 16	17 ------- 18	19
Rebid	Pass	No-trumps at lowest level over partner's new suit bid	No-trumps with jump over partner's new suit bid	3NT over partner's new suit bid

Opener is unbalanced:

1st option	Support responder with four cards – use Opener's Support Line			
	Points	Rule of 20 ------ 15	16 ------ 18	19
	Rebid	Support at lowest level	Support with a jump	Support to game

2nd option =	Rebid Six-card suit – use Opener's Six-card Repeat Line		
	Points	Rule of 20 ------- 15	16 ---------- 19
	Rebid	Repeat suit at lowest level	Repeat suit with a jump

2nd option =	Rebid new suit to show 5:4 – use Opener's 5:4 Line	
	Points	Rule of 20 -------------- 18	19
	Rebid	Bid second suit at lowest level	Bid second suit with a jump

Responder's rebid

By this stage the hard work has usually been done,
and responder can make a simple winning bid.
Assuming the auction began with a suit opener,
followed by a new suit response (from responder),
one of four things happened next:

(i) Opener rebid no-trumps.

(ii) Opener supported responder's suit.

(iii) Opener repeated his suit.

(iv) Opener bid a third suit.

Opener rebid no-trumps

By rebidding no-trumps, opener has described his strength to within narrow limits, putting responder in an excellent position. In most cases, responder will now know which zone the partnership is in (part-score, game or slam), and whether there's an eight-card major-suit fit.

Let's consider what you (as responder) should rebid with each of the following hands. In each case the bidding began 1♥-1♠-1NT (your partner opened 1♥, you responded 1♠, partner rebid 1NT – showing 15–16 points and a balanced hand).

(a)	(b)	(c)	(d)
♠ AQ10864	♠ Q1072	♠ KQ98	♠ KJ743
♥ 2	♥ J4	♥ K4	♥ Q94
♦ KJ52	♦ AQ92	♦ AJ72	♦ 32
♣ 83	♣ 865	♣ KQ3	♣ KJ4

(a) Rebid 4♠. Facing a partner who has advertised 15–16 points with at least two spades, the partnership has a spade fit, plus the values for game. Don't mess about – go straight there.

(b) Rebid 2NT. With one more point, you'd know game values were present and would bid 3NT. With one fewer point, you'd know game values weren't present and would pass opener's 1NT. Your rebid 2NT shows precisely nine points. Now all your partner needs to do is see whether he's minimum (15) or maximum (16) for his next bid.

(c) Rebid 6NT. Your 18 points added to your partner's minimum of 15 yields the 33 necessary for a no-trump slam. Bingo!

(d) Rebid 3♥. Game values are present but, as always, finding an eight-card major-suit fit should be your priority. Your partner may have five hearts and/or three spades. The jump to 3♥ announcing game values (2♥ would be weak) facilitates the finding of either fit, should it exist. Opener will raise to 4♥ if he has five hearts; with four hearts and three spades, he'll bid 3♠ (whereupon you'll raise to 4♠, as you have five), and with just two spades he'll bid 3NT. Note that your partner knows you don't have four-card heart support – or you'd have supported hearts immediately.

Opener supported responder's suit

This leaves responder in an excellent position. A fit has been found and she just needs to determine at which level to rebid – to go for game, slam or part-score. Point count is useful here, but sheer number of points shouldn't be the only focus; also consider: location of points (they're most valuable in long suits), hand distribution (a 5431 shape is much more powerful than a 4333), and degree of fit (we search for a suit with eight cards, but the ninth and tenth trumps can be invaluable).

Now consider the best rebid strategy (for you as responder) with the following hands. In each case the bidding has begun 1♦-1♠-2♠ (your partner opened 1♦, you responded 1♠, partner rebid 2♠ – showing a minimum-type opener with four card spade support).

(a)	(b)	(c)
♠ KQ982	♠ KJ1063	♠ A8642
♥ 4	♥ 4	♥ QJ3
♦ KQ3	♦ KQ2	♦ 763
♣ J932	♣ AQ42	♣ QJ

(a) Rebid 4♠. This is a great hand: a good shape with all your honours (except ♣J) working well, either in trumps or in your partner's diamonds. You should be disappointed to fail in game, even though there may not be 25 points.

(b) Rebid 4NT. Even better – another great shape, with honours in the right places. The only worry about a slam venture is the number of aces in your partner's hand. Your 4NT (Blackwood convention) bid asks your partner how many he holds. Provided he shows two (or three) aces, you should follow with 6♠. If he replies 5♦, indicating just one ace, then sign off in 5♠ (two missing aces).

must know
Never withhold primary (four-card) support for your partner's major suit. A fit in a major suit takes priority over everything (one fewer trick is required to make game than in a minor suit (see p. 221)).

(c) Pass. There may be 25 points (your partner's range is up to 15 points), but are those queen-jacks in your short suits really worth anything? If your partner has two small cards in hearts and clubs (perfectly possible), your 'quacks' may as well be low cards.

Opener repeated his suit

In this instance, opener will have used the 'Opener's Six-card Repeat Line' (see p. 175) to show in his rebid (i) his six-card suit, and (ii) his strength. Because responder needs only two cards to support opener, she'll normally have a fit for the suit. Then the only outstanding issue to resolve is level.

Let's consider what you (as responder) should rebid with the following hands. The bidding in each case began 1♥-1♠-2♥ (your partner opened 1♥, you responded 1♠, he rebid 2♥ – showing six hearts and up to 15 points).

(a)	(b)	(c)
♠ AK82	♠ J7632	♠ AJ92
♥ Q4	♥ J10	♥ 3
♦ KJ83	♦ K2	♦ Q1093
♣ 932	♣ AQ42	♣ KQJ3

(a) Rebid 4♥. You have a known eight-card heart fit, plus the values for game.

(b) Rebid 3♥. You have a known eight-card heart fit, and perhaps the values for game. 3♥ asks opener if he's minimum or maximum for his 12-15 point range.

(c) Rebid 3NT. You have the values for game, no major-suit fit, and good stoppers in three suits (your partner has your singleton suit well covered as you know he holds six cards).

Opener bid a third suit

In this fourth possible scenario, where the first three bids have all been in different suits, there's more work to be done. In each of the three scenarios described above, opener's rebid limited his point count to within a narrow range. But here, communicating a point count becomes the job of the responder. On the plus side, opener has shown his shape (five-four) so in most cases a fit will be evident.

Responder has three main options for her rebid (the other choice being a bid of the fourth suit). Support, as always, is the top priority:

> (i) Support one of opener's suits – preferably a major.
> (ii) Repeat responder's suit (responder must hold six cards in the suit).
> (iii) Bid no-trumps (responder must have a good stopper in the unbid suit).

In each case responder should show the strength of her hand through the level of her bid, using the 'Responder's Line' below as a guide. Note that when it comes to the point ranges, a bid of 1NT belongs to the 'Two level', 2NT to the 'Three level', etc (i.e. with, say, 6–9 points, responder would choose between the following bids: 1NT, 2♣, 2♦, 2♥ or 2♠; with 10–12, she would choose from 2NT, 3♣, 3♦, 3♥ or 3♠, etc).

must know
The Responder's Line (on this page) and the Responder's Support Line (on p. 65) are essentially the same line. Apart from bidding new suits, responder should always use this line: whether supporting her partner, repeating her own suit, or bidding no-trumps.

The Responder's Line

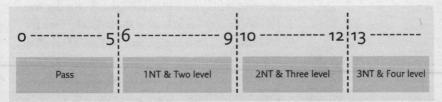

0 ----------- 5	6 ------------- 9	10 ----------- 12	13 --------
Pass	1NT & Two level	2NT & Three level	3NT & Four level

Now consider what you (as responder) should bid with the
following hands. In each case the bidding began 1♦-1♥-1♠ (your
partner opened 1♦, you responded 1♥, partner rebid 1♠ –
showing a five-four shape, but not limiting his strength).

(a)	(b)	(c)	(d)
♠ QJ4	♠ QJ72	♠ K3	♠ J74
♥ AJ862	♥ K974	♥ KQ10963	♥ QJ84
♦ Q92	♦ A52	♦ Q10	♦ A3
♣ 93	♣ 93	♣ 974	♣ QJ94

(a) Rebid 3♦. Your partner has advertised five diamonds and
four spades, so you have a diamond fit. Using the 'Responder's
Line', your 3♦ bid shows 10-12 points. Opener will pass if he
can't see game (Five of a minor normally requires 28 or 29
points), although he may think about 3NT if he has a good
stopper in clubs.

(b) Rebid 3♠. There are fits in both diamonds and spades, but
the major suit takes priority, as one fewer trick is required to
make game.

(c) Rebid 3♥. Repeating the suit shows you have six cards, and
bidding at the Three level (involving, here, a jump) shows your
10-12 points. A 2♥ rebid would show 6-9 points, and a good
game might be missed as a result.

(d) Rebid 2NT. No fit is evident, so, as you have a reasonable
holding in the unbid suit (clubs), you should offer no-trumps.
Your 2NT bid shows 10-12 points, indicating to opener how
much he needs for game.

Up to now we've focused our attention on the first
four partnership bids. With good reason: if these four
bids are correct – or at least in the ballpark – then the
final contract (if not already reached) will be sensible.
It's when one of these initial bids is wrong that the
final contract is likely to be seriously askew. Then
there can be chaos!

There's another potential cause of chaos: the disruptive influence of the opponents. We can't always assume they will be silent.

Coping with opposing intervention

In the previous pages covering the first four partnership bids we've assumed your opponents to be silent in the bidding. Of course the opponents don't have to bid (for when to overcall or double see pp. 37–9, 71–7 and 126–37). But what happens when your right-hand opponent *does* make a bid? Does our code disintegrate? Not at all. If you were planning to make a bid to show ('limit') the strength of your hand (i.e. not a new-suit bid), then you should go ahead with your bid, assuming you can do so. Otherwise, you should pass and see if your partner can bid.

Coping with opposing interference

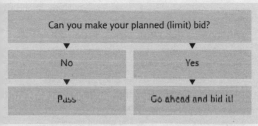

Can you make your planned (limit) bid?	
▼	▼
No	Yes
▼	▼
Pass	Go ahead and bid it!

Here are some examples:

(a) With the following hand you opened 1♥, your partner responded 1♠, and then your right-hand opponent overcalled 2♣. What next?

♠ K7
♥ AK75
♦ QJ63
♣ Q86

Answer:
You must pass. You can no longer make your planned rebid of 1NT, and to stretch to 2NT would show 17–18 points (too many). However don't worry unduly as your partner still has another bid. He should realize that your rebid has been taken away (or you'd simply have made it) and deduce that your plan must have been to rebid 1NT or 2♣, the only two bids that your right-hand opponent's intervention prevented.

(b) With the following hand you opened 1NT, your partner responded 2♣ (the Stayman convention – a request for four-card majors – see p. 164), and your right-hand opponent put in a bid of 2♠. What should you bid next?

♠ K73
♥ AJ75
♦ KJ63
♣ J6

Answer:
You must pass. You were planning to reply 2♥, but as this is no longer possible, you must now keep quiet. Your partner wouldn't thank you for bidding 3♥ if he has a 'Phoney Stayman' hand, with six clubs and nothing else (see p. 167). Note that if your majors were swapped, and the over-call had been 2♥, you could now make the 2♠ bid you were planning to make, and should go ahead and do so.

(c) With the following hand you opened 1♦, your left-hand opponent overcalled 1♥, your partner responded 1♠, and your right-hand opponent supported the overcall with 2♥. What should you bid now?

♠ K7
♥ Q5
♦ KJ8432
♣ AJ5

Answer:
You must pass because you're unable to make your planned rebid. (You were planning to rebid 2♦, showing up to 15 points and implying a six-card diamond suit.) To bid 3♦ would show 16+ points and a good six-card suit. If you had ♦Q instead of ♥Q you might have considered stretching things a little with a 3♦ bid in order to show your rebiddable diamond suit. However with your actual hand, ♥Q is likely to be worthless in the light of the opposing heart bidding. A 3♦ bid would be an overstatement of your values

Understanding contested auctions

In a contested auction when you are trying to understand the meaning of your partner's bid – or, indeed, the meaning of your intended response – the best approach is to strip away the opposing bids and consider the auction as an uncontested bidding sequence.

For instance, in the auction where you opened 1♦, your left-hand opponent overcalled 1♥, your partner responded 1♠, and your right-hand opponent supported the overcall with 2♥, to understand the message attached to your partner's bid, consider the sequence instead as: 1♦-pass-1♠-pass, i.e. with the opposing bids stripped away. The message will be much clearer.

must know

In a contested auction, be most concerned about a Double, the most serious competitive bid, which may lead to your opponents winning the contract. Your opponents' overcalls, on the other hand, are designed partly to disrupt you and your partner's bidding sequence.

Evaluating a bridge hand

Our primary method of evaluating the worth of your hand during this book has been counting high-card points. For a method so simple, it's a surprisingly good predictor of the power of your hand. However it is far from giving you the full picture.

Assessing your hand

Here are some factors ignored by the point-count scheme:

• **Intermediate cards:** Particularly in no-trumps, tens and nines are very valuable.

For example, contrast the following two 1NT openers:

(a)	(b)
♠ K1093	♠ K643
♥ Q10	♥ Q3
♦ AJ109	♦ AJ43
♣ K108	♣ K54

(a) looks (and is) much more powerful than (b). If your partner bid 2NT, to invite you to game, you should accept by bidding 3NT with (a), yet pass with (b).

• **Sequential high cards:** Having honours in sequence is very powerful, and it's far preferable to have adjacent honours in the same hand.

For example, contrast (a) and (b):

(a)	(b)
♣ KQ2	♣ K32
facing	facing
♣ 543	♣ Q54

With precisely the same high cards in both scenarios, in (a) you (as declarer) have a 50-50 chance of promoting both the king and queen – by leading twice from the opposite hand, in the hope that the ace is positioned in front of the king-queen. In (b), you have next to no chance of promoting both club honours. Wherever the ace is positioned, you'll have to sacrifice one of the honours to force out the ace and promote the other.

• Honours in your long suits: Honours are much more likely to pull their weight when accompanied by low cards.

For example, consider which is a more powerful diamond holding between hands (a) and (b):

(a)	(b)
♦ AKJ32	♦ J5432
facing	facing
♦ 54	♦ AK

(a) offers far better trick-taking chances for two reasons: firstly you can hope to promote the jack (via a finesse, leading from the opposite hand); secondly, the blockage in (b) renders the setting up of long cards problematic because of the resulting entry difficulties.

• Shape: We've seen the importance of shape throughout this book, with a preference for hand-patterns with disparate suit lengths such as 5431, compared to the sterile 4333.

must know
A balanced hand has roughly the same number of cards In each suit. An unbalanced hand has one or two suits longer than the other suits. A balanced hand suggests a no-trump contract because no one suit dominates. An unbalanced hand suggests one of the long suits as a trump suit.

must know

When the opponents have bid and supported a suit, ask yourself whether you have the right number of cards in their suit. For example, a distribution of one/four cards between you and your partner, rather than two/three, ensures the opposition make a minimum number of tricks in their suit (see the example at the foot of p.194).

In the following somewhat extreme example (a) offers rather better trick-taking chances than (b), although they both have ten points and one card of each rank:

(a)	(b)
♠ AKQJ1098765432	♠ A642
♥ –	♥ K108
♦ –	♦ Q95
♣ –	♣ J73

Making a much smaller difference, contrast (c) and (d) below:

(c)	(d)
♠ 2	♠ 62
♥ KJ1063	♥ KJ103
♦ AQ97	♦ AQ97
♣ J85	♣ J85

The only difference between the two hands is ♥6 in (c) becomes ♠6 in (d), and yet this is enough to transform the hand. (c) is an opening hand with an easy bidding strategy (open 1♥, then rebid 2♦ to show the 5-4 shape). (d) is much less exciting – a balanced hand with insufficient values to open.

Listening to the bidding

When the bidding gets underway, you must reassess your hand with each piece of new information. Again, point count only tells a small part of the story.

For example, look at these two similar hands belonging to responder:

(a)	(b)
♠ A865	♠ A865
♥ 1096	♥ 1096
♦ KQ2	♦ 753
♣ 753	♣ KQ2

On both occasions the bidding proceeds:

Opener	Responder (you)
1♥	1♠
2♦	?

Your partner (opener) has shown at least five hearts and four diamonds, so it's clear you need to revert to hearts. Thinking only in terms of high-card points, you'd bid 2♥ with both hands (a) and (b) to show your 6–9 points. Let's now look at opener's hand to see if 2♥ is the correct bid:

> Opener's hand
> ♠ 94
> ♥ AKQ53
> ♦ AJ64
> ♣ 86

Opener would undoubtedly pass 2♥, knowing that he faces just 6–9 points (and the possibility of responder having only two hearts and being some-what stuck for a rebid). 2♥ is the correct contract facing responder's hand (b) – which rates to make eight or nine tricks, but almost never ten. However facing responder's hand (a), an easy 4♥ game has been missed: assuming a reasonable trump split, there are five trumps, four diamonds and ♣A to win.

The nub is this: hand (a)'s ♠K and ♠Q become promoted in value because they face opener's length in diamonds. The upgrading of these cards enables the hand to rebid, not 2♥, but 3♥. This rebid shows 10–12 points, which is what the hand is now worth. Over the 3♥ rebid, opener would continue to 4♥ and game would be reached.

qually, you need to upgrade or downgrade your hand
ccording to what you learn from the opposition.

Consider which of the following two hands belonging to you as opener (South) is more powerful:

(a)	(b)
♠ AK532	♠ AK532
♥ K2	♥ 432
♦ 432	♦ K2
♣ AJ2	♣ AJ2

In each case, the bidding has progressed:

must know

Remember to downgrade high honours (especially kings) in suits bid by your left-hand opponent, and upgrade high honours in suits bid by your right-hand opponent.

South (you)	West	North	East
1♠	2♥	2♠	3♦
?			

With West (your left-hand opponent) likely to have ♥A, and East (your right-hand opponent) ♦A, you'd much prefer to hold hand (b). Your ♦K is likely to score a trick, and any heart honours your partner holds will be well placed. You can compete to 3♠, and expect to make it.

Hand (a) is a different story. ♥K is sitting under your left-hand opponent's (West's) ♥A, and any honours your partner holds in diamonds are sitting under East's honours. You can anticipate the play starting with a diamond lead from West, East scoring the first two or three tricks in the suit, then switching to a heart through your king. You'd be lucky to get even close to 3♠, and should certainly pass 3♦.

Now consider which is the most powerful of the following three hands belonging to you as opener (South):

(a)	(b)	(c)
♠ AQ86	♠ AQ86	♠ AQ86
♥ 42	♥ Q2	♥ 432
♦ 42	♦ 42	♦ 2
♣ AK953	♣ AK953	♣ AK943

In each case, the bidding has progressed:

South (you)	West	North	East
1♣	1♥	1♠	3♥
?			

Think about the implications of the bidding before simply counting points and assuming (b) is the most powerful hand. The opponents have bid to the Three level in their overcalled suit (hearts), so you can assume they have a nine-card fit (over-callers tend to bid to the 'level of their fit' – see p. 74).

The most powerful hand is (c). With three hearts in your hand, you can deduce that your partner is likely to have just one (or none at all), given the 3♥ bid by

East. Thus with ten of the opponents' points (♥AKQJ) likely to take at most one trick against your contract (your partner's hand would void of hearts after one trick, after which you could trump), you won't need anything like 25 points to make game. You should jump to 4♠.

With hand (a), you're pleased to have a spade fit, and to have all the honours in your long suits. However, the fact that your partner is also likely to have two hearts should steer you away from the bold leap to 4♠ (the opposition would stand to make two tricks in hearts). You should be content with a bid of 3♠.

Hand (b) is two points stronger than the others – or is it? ♥Q is almost certainly worthless against the opposition's honours cards, and should be discounted. In fact there's an argument that, because the opponents have bid to 3♥ without ♥Q, they may have some compensating values elsewhere that could do you some damage, so you would actually prefer not to have ♥Q. In this sense, hand (b) is worse than hand (a), in spite of holding more points. (An interesting case of more being less!) You'd nonetheless bid 3♠ (but not even consider 4♠).

The more you play bridge, the less you'll rely on high-card points as a method of evaluating your hand, and the more you'll think about other factors, such as shape, intermediate cards and location of honours. You'll then constantly reassess your hand as the bidding progresses and more information is known. Below is a summary of the factors to consider when assessing your hand.

Points are a fair guide to hand evaluation, but don't be a slave to them. Bridge is about tricks, not points. Consider these other factors, both as you pick up your hand and as the auction progresses.

Factor	✔ (positive factor present)	✘ (negative factor present)
Honours in long suits?	KQ432	KQ
Even if balanced, do you have length?	5-3-3-2	4-3-3-3
Disparity of lengths?	5-4-3-1	4-4-4-1
Intermediates?	Q1092	Q532
At least one ace?	Aces	No ace
Rebid?	5♠ 4♥	4♠ 5♥
Sequential honours?	KQ2	AJ2
Well-placed honours?	In your partner's or right-hand opponent's suit	In your left-hand opponent's suit
Right number of cards in opponents' suit?	one/four cards	two-three cards

Ten developing deals

Example A

Dealer West

		North	
		♠ Q754	
		♥ AQJ5	
West		♦ AK6	East
♠ J6		♣ 85	♠ 10983
♥ K108			♥ 3
♦ QJ10			♦ 9832
♣ AKJ76		South	♣ 10432
		♠ AK2	
		♥ 97642	
		♦ 754	
		♣ Q9	

The bidding:

South	West	North	East
	1♣ (i)	Double (ii)	Pass
2♥ (iii)	Pass	4♥ (iv)	End

(i) West has a balanced hand but, too strong to open 1NT, starts with 1♣ and plans to rebid no-trumps. A plan that will soon have to be scrapped ...

(ii) Take-out, showing support for all unbid suits, opening values and shortage in the suit bid.

(iii) Jumping a level to show nine+ points (the key bid).

(iv) Knows from partner's jump that there is enough strength for game.

The play:

West cashes ♣A, (perhaps ♣K), and switches to ♦Q (in truth, he should probably switch to this card at Trick Two). Winning dummy's ♦K, you as declarer want to avoid a trump loser, via a finesse against West's hoped-for ♥K (he is the opening bidder after all). So cross to your ♠K, and lead ♥2, to ♥8, and ♥J. The finesse successful, you now need to repeat the finesse, in order to promote ♥Q. So cross back to your ♠A, and lead ♥4, to ♥10, and ♥Q. Cash ♥A, and you have picked up the trumps without loss.

The game is now secure, but, trying for an overtrick, you cash ♠Q. If the suit splits three-three, you are in a position to enjoy ♠7, a length winner. But East (who does well to stay interested holding, as he does, such a meagre collection), clings hold of all his spades (discarding clubs on the second and third round of trumps). In this way, East can beat dummy's ♠7 with ♠10, and you are held to ten tricks (losing a third round of diamonds at the end). Game made.

If you remember just one thing about ...

Bidding: With nine+ points facing a take-out double, you must jump the bidding.
Declaring. When finessing, lead from the opposite hand to the honour or honours you are trying to promote.
Defending: When discarding, keep equal length with dummy.

Example B

Dealer East

```
                    North
                    ♠ KJ9
                    ♥ 653
      West          ♦ 762          East
      ♠ 65          ♣ KJ109        ♠ AQ1073
      ♥ Q1097                      ♥ 4
      ♦ A53                        ♦ K84
      ♣ A754        South          ♣ Q862
                    ♠ 842
                    ♥ AKJ82
                    ♦ QJ109
                    ♣ 3
```

The bidding:

South	West	North	East
			1♠ (i)
2♥ (ii)	Double (iii)	Pass	Pass (iv)
Pass			

(i) Rule of 20. East opens happily, given the nice five-card spade suit.
(ii) Perfectly normal overcall, satisfying SQOT, and with the pleasing 5431 shape.
(iii) For penalties – as his partner has bid. West has two trump tricks – satisfying the Penalty Double Rule (see figure on p. 133) – plus two aces. That's four defensive tricks. Surely he can rely on his partner for at least two more. West reasons that he can defeat 2♥, and may well have no game contract.
(iv) You need a much more shapely hand to think about removing partner's penalty double, such as a void heart and/or a six-five shape.

The play:

West leads ♠6 to dummy's ♠9 (it doesn't matter), and East wins ♠10. East does not cash ♠A (promoting dummy's ♠K). Instead he switches to ♦4 (dummy's weakness), to ♦A. West reverts to ♠5, crucially leading through ♠KJ, and East beats ♠J with ♠Q, and cashes ♠A. West discards ♦3, such that East can now cash ♦K and lead ♦8 for West to 'ruff' (i.e. trump).

The defence has won the first six tricks, so a happy West now cashes ♣A and waits to score one further trump trick with ♥Q109. Down three and East-West +800.

If you remember just one thing about ...

Bidding: The Penalty Double Rule.
Declaring: If you can't do anything about it, there is no point in ruing the play.
Defending: Do not promote unnecessary winners in dummy (such as, in this example, ♠K).

Example C

Dealer West

	North	
	♠ 43	
	♥ AQ9	
West	♦ KJ1092	East
♠ QJ10	♣ AK4	♠ K9875
♥ KJ54		♥ 1063
♦ A73		♦ 4
♣ J96	South	♣ 10752
	♠ A62	
	♥ 872	
	♦ Q865	
	♣ Q83	

The bidding:

South	West	North	East
	1NT	Double (i)	2♠ (ii)
2NT (iii)	Pass	3NT (iv)	End

(i) Penalties – showing 16+ points (any shape).
(ii) Rescuing into a five-card suit.
(iii) Tricky bid, but South knows partnership almost has the points for game, and he is balanced with a spade stopper.
(iv) Close – because he has just one more point than a minimum. But his five-card diamond suit looks good for tricks, and he knows that his partner will be able to place the missing high-cards (with West).

The play:

West leads ♠Q – top of a sequence in his partner's five-card suit. Should you as declarer win your ♠A? The reason for withholding (ducking) your ace is to exhaust West of his spades. When he wins a subsequent lead, he will not have any more spades to lead to his partner. Let's see how it works.

You duck ♠A at Trick One, and again at Trick Two when West follows with ♠J. You win ♠A at Trick Three, and are confident that West has no more spades (East showed five in the bidding). You now lead ♦Q and, when West wins ♦A (if he ducks, then you lead diamonds until he is forced to take his ace), he has no spade to lead. Say he switches to ♥4. You can rise with ♥A, cash the promoted diamonds, and follow with the three top clubs. Nine tricks and game made.

Note for the overtrick-hungry amongst you (and those with aspirations to Duplicate Bridge should take note, as overtricks are very valuable in that form of the game): West must hold ♥K to justify his 1NT opener (count the missing high-card points). So you can safely finesse ♥Q on his ♥4 return at Trick Five. This ensures a tenth trick.

If you remember just one thing about ...

Bidding: The double of 1NT is for penalties – showing any hand with 16+ points.
Declaring: In no trumps, withhold ('duck') your one certain stopper, until you have exhausted an opponent of their cards in the suit.
Defending: Do not always lead 'fourth highest of your longest suit' against no-trumps. Remember the bidding.

Example D

Dealer South

```
                    North
                    ♠ AKJ
                    ♥ AQJ
        West        ♦ Q1054      East
        ♠ 872       ♣ Q62        ♠ Q954
        ♥ 108532                 ♥ 76
        ♦ A9                     ♦ 8763
        ♣ J95       South        ♣ 1084
                    ♠ 1063
                    ♥ K94
                    ♦ KJ2
                    ♣ AK73
```

The bidding:

South	West	North	East
1NT	Pass	4NT (i)	Pass
6NT (ii)	End		

(i) Small slam invite in no-trumps – are you minimum or maximum? If maximum, we have the 33 points we need.
(ii) Maximum – 14 points.

The play:

West would tend to lead an ace (even without the king) against a trump slam; but there is more time against a no-trump slam, and to take only low cards would be poor use of an ace. West leads ♥3. You, as declarer, count up eight top tricks, but know that you can easily generate three more by forcing out ♦A.

You win ♥J, and lead ♦4 to ♦K. West wins ♦A, and leads a second heart. You are just one trick short now – with your three promoted force winners in diamonds. Where is the twelfth trick coming from?

There are two possibilities:
(a) It could come from the spade finesse – leading to dummy's ♠J, and hoping West holds ♠Q (an even money chance). Or
(b) It could come from a fourth-round club length winner, should the six opposing clubs split three-three.

Whilst (b) is less likely (a missing even number of cards do not usually split evenly), nonetheless you should test clubs first. Why?

Answer: Should the suit fail to split evenly, you still have the spade finesse in reserve: in other words you can test both your options. The problem with taking the spade finesse before testing clubs is that, if a spade to the jack loses to ♠Q, you are down (a second trick to the defence).

So win the second heart and lead out ♣Q and over to ♣AK. The suit does split three-three, so you can now enjoy the thirteenth club length winner, discarding ♠J. It is now a simple matter to cash the remaining heart, three promoted diamonds, and ♠AK. 12 tricks and small slam made.

If you remember just one thing about ...

Bidding. If partner's last bid is no trumps, 4NT is a no trump slam invite (not an ace ask).
Declaring: With a choice of methods of making extra tricks, finessing is typically the last resort (because a losing finesse often spells irrevocable failure).
Defending: Cash an unsupported ace against a suit slam, but not a no-trump slam.

Example E

Dealer South

```
                      North
                      ♠ 763
                      ♥ 65
        West          ♦ A743          East
        ♠ 842         ♣ 7632          ♠ 9
        ♥ KJ103                       ♥ A984
        ♦ Q10                         ♦ K9852
        ♣ QJ109       South           ♣ 854
                      ♠ AKQJ105
                      ♥ Q72
                      ♦ J6
                      ♣ AK
```

The bidding:

South	West	North	East
2♠ (i)	Pass	2NT (ii)	Pass
3♠ (iii)	Pass	4♠ (iv)	End

(i) Around 20–22 points and an unbalanced hand with a good five – or preferably six – card suit.
(ii) Negative – up to seven points.
(iii) Non-forcing – 'if you are bereft, partner, I'm happy to play in part-score'.
(iv) An ace, three trumps and 'ruffing value' (i.e. trumping potential) in hearts: a clear 4♠ bid.

The play:

West leads ♣Q and you as declarer count nine tricks. Needing one more, you notice that dummy has fewer hearts than you – crucial in a trump contract (see p. 87). You win ♣K, and lead a heart (key play), in order to void dummy of hearts whilst trumps are still held.

The defence win the heart, and switch to a trump, in an attempt to remove dummy's trumps (West reflecting that an – unlikely – trump lead would have worked well). You win and lead a second heart, thus voiding the dummy of hearts. West wins and leads a second trump. You win, and can now make your extra trick: in spite of the defence's best efforts, you still hold one trump in dummy. That card is about to make a trick in its own right: you lead your third heart, and 'ruff' (i.e. trump) with it. Extra trick: you now cross to ♣A, draw West's last trump, and nine tricks have become ten.

If you remember just one thing about ...

Bidding: Remember the 2NT 'no slam' negative response to a 2♦/♥/♠ opener.

Declaring: In a trump contract, look for a side-suit shorter in dummy than in hand. If so, try to void that suit and trump extra card(s) before drawing trumps.

Defending: If you see declarer voiding dummy of a side-suit before drawing your trumps, then switch to a trump.

Example F

Dealer East

	North	
	♠ AQ1062	
	♥ AKJ	
West	♦ J954	East
♠ 9754	♣ A	♠ 8
♥ 6		♥ 873
♦ AK83		♦ 102
♣ 10862	South	♣ KQJ9543
	♠ KJ3	
	♥ Q109542	
	♦ Q76	
	♣ 7	

The bidding:

South	West	North	East
			3♣ (i)
Pass (ii)	5♣ (iii)	Double (iv)	Pass
5♥ (v)	End		

(i) Pre-emptive. Less than an opening hand, with a good seven-card suit.

(ii) Bidding over an opposing pre-empt shows a near-opening hand or better.

(iii) Knowing his partnership hold 11 clubs, West bids to the 'level of the fit'. With good support (plus a side-suit singleton), West thinks that 5♣ will be a good sacrifice against an opposing heart game.

(iv) Essentially for take-out, but partner will often play for three tricks on defence at this high level (by passing, effectively converting the double into penalties).

(v) With a decent six-card heart suit, it is reasonable to try for the 11-trick contract. Indeed, had South passed and opted to defend, he would defeat East (in 5♣ doubled) by just one trick (scoring a spade, a heart and ♣A, but nothing else).

The play:

West leads ♦A, the best opening lead against a trump contract. Holding third-round control (i.e. a doubleton), East signals 'throw high means aye' by playing ♦10. West then cashes ♦K, and leads a third diamond. East ruffs. You as declarer can win any return, draw trumps, and claim the remainder, but you are down one.

If you remember just one thing about ...

Bidding: When bidding to spoil, bid to the level of the fit.

Declaring: Did you think about playing ♦Q under ♦A at Trick One? Cost-nothing foxing opportunities like that can lead the opponents astray.

Defending: If partner leads an ace against a trump contract, normally you should signal encouragement ('throw high means aye') when you hold the queen, or a doubleton (i.e. third-round control).

Example G

Dealer South

```
                    North
                    ♠ A3
                    ♥ AK64
    West            ♦ A3            East
    ♠ 5             ♣ 108753        ♠ K76
    ♥ QJ102                         ♥ 8753
    ♦ KJ95                          ♦ Q1076
    ♣ Q962          South           ♣ AK
                    ♠ QJ109842
                    ♥ 9
                    ♦ 842
                    ♣ J4
```

The bidding:

South	West	North	East
3♠ (i)	Pass (ii)	4♠ (iii)	End

(i) Pre-emptive, and bottom of the range! You are showing less than an opening hand with a good seven-card suit. Here – much less.
(ii) Perfect shape for a take-out double, but about an ace short of opening values.
(iii) Four wonderful quick tricks. A pre-emptor can normally make about six tricks from his hand (hmmm), to bring the total to the required ten.

The play:

West leads ♥Q, and your frisky pre-empt will pay off nicely if you play well. Pleased to have avoided an (impossible to find) opening trump lead from West, you win ♥K, and immediately cash ♥A, throwing a club. You do not throw a diamond because, in effect, your third diamond is a winner. The reason for this is our old favourite: dummy having fewer cards in a side-suit to us. And that's the basis of our strategy here.

At Trick Three cash ♦A, and follow with ♦3. The defence is best for West to win the second diamond, and fire through ♠5. If you play low, you risk East winning ♠K, and leading a second trump. This would remove both of dummy's trumps before your third diamond has been trumped. So you rise with ♠A, ruff a third heart (to get back to hand), then, the crucial extra trick, lead the third diamond and ruff it with dummy's small trump. Your remaining ♠QJ1098 are equals against ♠K, so you must score four more tricks. 10 tricks and game made. The key was ruffing the third diamond in dummy.

If you remember just one thing about ...

Bidding: It is clear to raise a 3♥/♠ opener to game holding four quick tricks. Even less - opening points in aces and kings - may give game a good chance (see p. 152).

Declaring: If you are trying to ruff in dummy, you cannot afford to have all dummy's trumps removed.

Defending: When you and partner have a choice of which player wins (such as the second round of diamonds), think to the next trick. Which defender can do more damage with his next lead?

Example H

Dealer South

```
                    North
                    ♠ A1096
                    ♥ 65
        West        ♦ Q7            East
        ♠ 8753      ♣ AK843         ♠ 4
        ♥ Q10                       ♥ KJ984
        ♦ AJ4                       ♦ K10852
        ♣ J1096     South           ♣ 52
                    ♠ KQJ2
                    ♥ A732
                    ♦ 963
                    ♣ Q7
```

The bidding:

South	West	North	East
1NT	Pass	2♣ (i)	Pass
2♥ (ii)	Pass	3NT (iii)	Pass
4♠ (iv)	End		

(i) The Stayman convention – a request for four-card major suits.

(ii) Showing four hearts (also possibly four spades).

(iii) Correct to assume partner does not have four spades – if he does then he has a further obligation ...

(iv) Knowing partner has four spades – he would not bid Stayman without either four-card major. Even though you are balanced, you must remove 3NT into 4♠. Partner's 2♣ bid, in effect, says, 'I want to play in a major-suit, should a fit exist'.

The play:

West leads ♣J against 4♠. Plan the play. One important area, with which we have not fully dealt, is using trumps to set up a long suit. Here is an example.

Win ♣Q and cash ♠KQ. When East discards, do not draw more trumps. Instead seek to establish dummy's five-card club suit. The suit could easily be four-two (the likeliest split), in which case you will need to trump a round. Lead your second club to ♣K, and then trump a low club (key play) with ♠J (another key play). West can only discard, so you cross to ♠A10, drawing West's trumps, cash ♣A, and then follow with the established ♣8 (thanks to your trumping a round). ♥A brings the trick total to ten – game made.

If you remember just one thing about ...

Bidding: The Stayman bidder should assume that a 2♥ reply does not also contain four spades. It is opener's duty to take the partnership back to spades should he happen to hold both four-card majors.

Declaring: Look for a five-card side-suit to set up. In a trump contract, this can be done by 'ruffing out the suit'. Normally, you will be well advised to address yourself to this task *before* drawing all the missing trumps.

Defending: Nothing specific to say, so I'll give you a tip that applies to every defence. When dummy is tabled, try to sense declarer's reaction. Is he happy? Unhappy? What do *you* think of dummy – if it is better than you thought, then desperate measures may be needed to defeat the contract.

Example I

Dealer North

```
                    North
                    ♠ AK65
                    ♥ J4
    West            ♦ 103            East
    ♠ J10           ♣ AK873          ♠ 9843
    ♥ Q1096                          ♥ 8
    ♦ KQJ4                           ♦ A8752
    ♣ J95           South            ♣ 1062
                    ♠ Q72
                    ♥ AK7532
                    ♦ 96
                    ♣ Q4
```

The bidding:

South	West	North	East
		1♣	Pass
1♥	Pass	1♠ (i)	Pass
3♥ (ii)	Pass	4♥ (iii)	End

(i) Showing (at least) a five-four shape.
(ii) The key bid. Using the Responder's Line (see p. 185), 10–12 points with six hearts (and presumably no black-suit fit).(iii) Knows of the eight-card heart fit, and that there is enough combinedstrength (15+10 points) for game.

The play:

West leads ♦K, follows with ♦Q (after ♦K wins the trick), and switches to ♠J. Your only problem as declarer is a four-one trump split. In that case it will be imperative to try to promote ♥J – catering to West holding four trumps headed by the queen. (Note that nothing can be done if East holds those trumps: if you make the mistake of actually leading ♥J, East will simply cover ♥J with ♥Q, and you have achieved nothing.)

In order to promote ♥J, you must lead from the opposite hand, and to this end you must win ♠J with ♠Q, and, without cashing either of ♥AK, lead a low trump (key play). Look at West's dilemma. He can play ♥Q, and take nothing with it (♥J, then ♥AK, will draw his three remaining trumps). Or he can play low, in which case dummy's ♥J will win the trick, and only the fourth round of trumps is lost. (See also the figure on p.169). With no other losers, that's ten tricks and game made.

Note that if a trump to ♥J lost to East's ♥Q, then you will still survive providing the suit split three-two (the remaining cards falling under your ♥AK). Leading a low heart to ♥J, rather than cashing ♥A first, is only wrong when East holds a singleton ♥Q. West holding four trumps headed by the queen is four times more likely.

If you remember just one thing about ...

Bidding: Remember to use the Responder's Line, when bidding old suits or no-trumps.
Declaring: Lead from the opposite hand to the card you're trying to promote. You cannot promote such a card as ♥J by actually leading it – whichever opponent holds the higher card (here ♥Q) will cover it.
Defending: Selecting the best opening lead is a combination of (i) listening to the bidding, and deciding which suit should be attacked; and (ii) looking at your hand, and seeing which is the most alluring holding to lead. When both answers point in the same direction, you have an easy choice. (Here diamonds is the unbid suit; and king-queen-jack is the most alluring holding.)

Example J

Dealer South

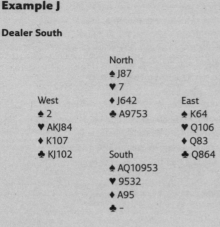

North
- ♠ J87
- ♥ 7
- ♦ J642
- ♣ A9753

West
- ♠ 2
- ♥ AKJ84
- ♦ K107
- ♣ KJ102

East
- ♠ K64
- ♥ Q106
- ♦ Q83
- ♣ Q864

South
- ♠ AQ10953
- ♥ 9532
- ♦ A95
- ♣ –

The bidding:

South	West	North	East
1♠ (i)	2♥ (ii)	2♠ (iii)	3♥ (iv)
4♠ (v)	End		

(i) A Rule of 20 opener – and what a powerful shape.

(ii) Prefer to overcall a decent five-card major, to making a take-out double.

(iii) The single-major raise showing 6–9 points – perfectly admissible without the fourth trump.

(iv) Known heart fit. Two-level overcalls should be raised with three cards wherever possible, even at the risk of going one beyond the level of the fit.

(v) The key bid. South knows from the opposing heart bidding that North has at most one heart. Therefore ten of the opponents' points (♥AKQJ) are taking at most one trick. North-South will not remotely need as many as 25 points to make game, backed up by the knowledge of the nine+ card fit.

The play:

West cashes ♥A and, looking at dummy's ruffing value, switches to his trump (best). You as declarer try dummy's ♠J, in the hope that East will cover with ♠K. The wily East is not to be tempted – there is no hope of his promoting a lower trump by doing so.

Now you are in a bind. If you use up a second trump in dummy to finesse East for ♠K, you will lose a heart ruff in dummy; yet if you use dummy's trumps to ruff two more hearts, you will be unable to finesse East for ♠K. Can you see a solution? You may find it easier to count potential winning tricks.

If you can score all your seven remaining trumps (in both hands), then the first round of trumps plus the two minor-suit aces will bring your trick total to ten. Although it is not normally correct to ruff in the long hand (unless setting up a suit), bridge has few hard-and-fast rules. Watch the elegance of the position that develops, as you ruff in both hands.

After winning ♠J, cash ♣A discarding (say) a heart. Then ruff a club, ruff a heart, ruff a club, ruff a heart, and ruff a club. Next cash ♦A (perhaps you should have cashed this card earlier), to bring about the following four card end-position:

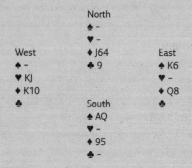

```
                    North
                    ♠ -
                    ♥ -
   West             ♦ J64          East
   ♠ -              ♣ 9            ♠ K6
   ♥ KJ                            ♥ -
   ♦ K10                           ♦ Q8
   ♣                               ♣
                    South
                    ♠ AQ
                    ♥ -
                    ♦ 95
                    ♣ -
```

With the lead in your hand, you need two more tricks. Exit with a diamond, and watch the defence cash two tricks in the suit. Your last two cards are now ♠AQ, sitting prettily over East's ♠K6. It doesn't matter which opponent is leading, you play ♠Q on East's ♠6 (or ♠A on his ♠K), and must score the last two tricks.

You scored all six trumps in your hand, two ruffs in dummy, and the two minor-suit aces. Total: ten tricks; and with just sixteen partnership points!

Being a good partner

One of the great joys of bridge is the partnership element. Be a good partner and your diary will soon fill up. Offer encouragement and you will get the best out of your partner, both in terms of their enjoyment and performance.

Good partnership guidelines

Here are eight of the most important guidelines for being a good partner, with the last being the most important of all.

- Always thank your partner for their dummy, even if it's a disappointment and/or you don't agree with their bidding.
- Never criticize your partner – remember they're trying their hardest.
- Congratulate your partner on a well played hand; commiserate them on a failed enterprise ('Hard luck' makes everyone feel better, even if luck didn't really come into it).
- Keep a straight face. Apart from being unethical to convey information through facial expression, it's also undermining.
- Try to picture things from your partner's side of the table – anticipate their problems and seek to make things clearer.
- Never side with an opponent against your partner. If you don't agree with your partner, say nothing.
- Always thank your partner at the end of the game (even if things didn't go well).

And finally...

> • Have a good time, and make sure that your partner does too.

As the US bridge legend Charles Goren said:

Bridge is for fun. You should play the game for no other reason. You should not play bridge to make money, to show how smart you are, or show how stupid your partner is or to prove any of the several hundred other things bridge players are so often trying to prove.

The late Rixi Markus – although never known for her gentleness at the bridge table – offered an excellent piece of advice for all bridge players when she said:

I have always believed that your attitude toward your partner is as important as your technical skill at the game.

> *English Lady International*

want to know more?
• Websites where you can play bridge are listed on p. 232.
• Computer software that offers practice and structured learning is listed on p. 232-3.
• Beginner-friendly bridge clubs are listed on p. 233.
• Books to help you develop your skills further are listed on p. 234-5.

5 Scoring and systems

Finally, we turn to methods of scoring bridge and, later in the chapter, some of the variants of the game and the different bidding styles. Scoring has been left until last because in fact you don't need to master the scoring in order to enjoy playing bridge. Indeed a game of bridge without anybody at all scoring, enjoying each deal for itself, can be a happy and worthwhile experience.

How to score bridge

The scoring set out here is for Rubber Bridge, the type of Contract Bridge described in this book and the one you are most likely to come across in a social setting.

must know
A rubber is the best of three games (scoring either 2-0 or 2-1 games wins a rubber). See pp. 221-2 for how to win a game.

Objective

The objective on each deal is for the declarer to make at least as many tricks as he contracted for in the bidding, and for his opponents (the defence) to try and prevent him. However, the overall objective for both sides is to score more points than the opposition and make game, as the first side to make two games wins the rubber, the ultimate goal.

The score-pad

First look at a typical score-pad (below). The first rubber is scored in the pair of columns on the left-hand side (headed 'We' and 'They'). The second

The score-pad (below) and where to put the scores (below right)

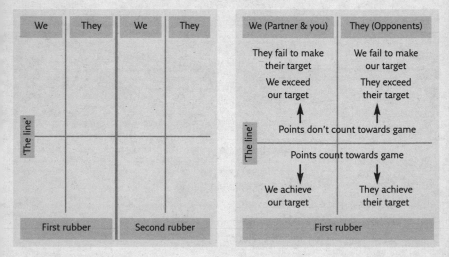

rubber is scored in the pair of columns on the right-hand-side (with the same headings). The horizontal line, slightly below half-way down, is a very important line. Only points below the line count towards game. Points above the line only count when the rubber has been won, whereupon all scores (below and above) are added up.

The scores

Here are the scores for Rubber Bridge:

Game: 100 points* are needed to make game. Tricks that are bid and made (above the first six) score points towards game as follows:

Minor suits (♦, ♣): Diamonds and clubs score 20 points per trick (above the first six tricks).

Major suits (♠, ♥): Spades and hearts score 30 points per trick (above the first six tricks).

No-trumps (NT): Score 40 points for the first trick (above the first six tricks) and 30 thereafter.

The bids required to make game in one deal are as follows:

Game contract		No. tricks required		Points made	
3NT	3 No-trumps	=	9 tricks	40+30+30	= 100
4♠	4 Spades	=	10 tricks	30 x 4	= 120
4♥	4 Hearts	=	10 tricks	30 x 4	= 120
5♦	5 Diamonds	=	11 tricks	20 x 5	= 100
5♣	5 Clubs	=	11 tricks	20 x 5	= 100

* NB: Don't confuse these scoring 'points' with the points you use to evaluate your hand.

Game

Game can be achieved in a single deal, or by adding together two or more part-scores. For example, if you bid and make 2♠ (eight tricks), scoring 60, then, on a subsequent deal, you bid and make 1NT (seven

5 Scoring and systems

must know

You become vulnerable when you win a game. You'll then concede 100 points per trick if you fail in a subsequent contract, compared to the 50 you'd lose if you failed before you won a game.

tricks), scoring 40, the scores added together make 100, which is game. But beware: if you make a part-score, but before you've been able to convert it to game by scoring again your opponents bid and make a game, then your part-score will no longer count towards a game. Although your part-score won't be erased (no scores are ever eliminated), you'll have to start the next game from zero (as will your opponents). Thus it pays to be bold and bid a game at one go if you think you have a fair chance to make it.

A partnership that has bid and made a game is termed 'vulnerable'. If both sides have made a game each, then both partnerships are vulnerable.

Undertricks

If you as declarer fail to make the number of tricks your side has contracted to make, then your side doesn't score any points, and your opponents score 'penalty points' instead. Penalty points go above the line, i.e. don't count towards game. If you aren't vulnerable, the defence scores 50 penalty points for each insufficient trick, but if you are vulnerable, each insufficient trick is worth 100 penalty points to the defence.

must know

When 'vulnerable', the incentive to bid game is greater (so be bold). But be more cautious when your bid might fail heavily (the result could be costly, especially, when the bid has been doubled – see p. 224).

Overtricks

If you make more tricks than you contracted for, then you score these 'overtricks' at the normal trick value and the score goes above the line (i.e. not counting towards game). Thus bidding 2♥ and making nine tricks scores 60 'below' and 30 'above'.

Winning the rubber

Like Wimbledon ladies' tennis, a rubber is the best of three games ('sets' at Wimbledon). If you're the first side to win two games (the rubber) then you get a bonus: 700 points if the opponents didn't get a game (i.e. 2-0 game score), and 500 points if they achieved one game (i.e. 2-1). To calculate the overall scores, add up the two columns ignoring the horizontal line. Subtract the smaller score from the larger and round to the nearest 100. Say your total score is 1,150 points and the opponents' is 320, you win by 830, which, rounded down to 800, makes an 'eight-point rubber'. Note that a difference of 60 or above is rounded up to the next 100, and 50 or below is rounded down. It's possible to be the first side to win two games (and therefore the bonus for winning the rubber) yet lose overall on points. This may happen, for instance, when your opponents bid a slam and/or you lose a doubled contract badly.

Score summary (left) and a sample rubber (right)

We	They
Bonus for winning the rubber: 700 (Two games to Zero) 500 (Two games to One)	
Undertricks count 50 points per trick (100 if 'vulnerable' i.e. if you have won a game)	
Overtricks score at trick value (NTs, ♠, ♥ =30; ♦, ♣ = 20)	
NTs = 40 points 1st trick 30 points each subsequent trick	
♠ ♥ ('Majors') = 30 points	
♦ ♣ ('Minors') = 20 points	
Game = 100 points below line Rubber = Best of three games	
Game contracts are 3NT, 4♥, 4♠, 5♣, 5♦	

We	They
500 (7)	
20 (7)	200 (6)
50 (3)	20 (5)
30 (2)	90 (4)
60 (1)	
60 (2)	
	120 (4)
100 (7)	40 (5)

Deal (1) We bid 2♠ and made eight tricks
Deal (2) We bid 2♥ and made nine tricks
Deal (3) They bid 4♥ and made nine tricks
Deal (4) They bid 1♠ and made all thirteen tricks
Deal (5) They bid 2♦ and made nine tricks
Deal (6) We bid 3♣ and made seven tricks
Deal (7) We bid 5♦ and made twelve tricks
We win the rubber and get a 500 bonus for winning 2-1

For those who like a modest stake (not necessary at all for the enjoyment of the game), say ten pence a hundred, then (in an eight-point rubber example) each member of 'They' would give 80 pence to each member of 'We'. You can then re-draw for partners or play another rubber with the same partner. For the new rubber, start a fresh pair of columns on the score-pad.

A score summary is set out on p. 223. Refer to this as you work through the sample rubber on the same page. Note that the sample rubber involves playing seven deals before one side ('We') wins the rubber with a 2-1 game score.

Scoring doubles

A contract that is doubled will score more points to the declaring side if it's successful, and more points to the defending side if it's unsuccessful.

Doubled undertricks

Your doubled undertricks (i.e. when your contract has gone down) are scored above the line in the column 'They'. These scores vary depending on how many you were down, and whether or not you were vulnerable – see the table below.

Scoring of doubled contracts that 'go down' (fail)

	Undoubled		Doubled	
	not Vul	Vul	not Vul	Vul
1 down	50	100	100	200
2 down	100	200	300	500
3 down	150	300	500	800
4 down	200	400	800	1100
5 down	250	500	1100	1400
	Vul = Vulnerable			

Doubled contracts that make

In cases where you successfully make a contract that has been doubled, the score below the line in the column 'We' is doubled – thus 60 points becomes 120 ('doubled into game'). You also get an extra 50 points 'for the insult', which goes above the line.

Any doubled overtricks score at 100 each if not vulnerable and 200 each if vulnerable.

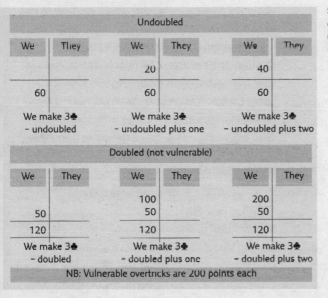

Scoring of doubled contracts that 'make' (are successfully fulfilled)

Undoubled					
We	They	We	They	We	They
			20		40
60		60		60	
We make 3♣ – undoubled		We make 3♣ – undoubled plus one		We make 3♣ – undoubled plus two	

Doubled (not vulnerable)					
We	They	We	They	We	They
		100		200	
50		50		50	
120		120		120	
We make 3♣ – doubled		We make 3♣ – doubled plus one		We make 3♣ – doubled plus two	
NB: Vulnerable overtricks are 200 points each					

Redoubled contracts

A contract that is redoubled (see p. 137) will score exactly twice (both above and below the line) that of a doubled contract. The game, rubber and slam bonuses remain the same.

Scoring slams

Bidding and making 'Six of something' (a small slam) or 'Seven of something' (a grand slam) is a gamble.

5 Scoring and systems

Slam bonuses

Scoring bonus	Small slam	Grand slam
Not vulnerable	500	1000
Vulnerable	750	1500

You score no points at all for failure – even by one trick. But, as we saw in chapter 4, the bonuses for success are great (see the table left). Note that you score substantially more when vulnerable (i.e. you have already won a game). With so much to gain for success, you may think you should be bolder in bidding slams when vulnerable. However, failure will cost you a vulnerable game, which in turn is worth more than a non-vulnerable game. In other words, you have more to gain, but more to lose.

The diagram below shows four scenarios illustrating the effects of being bold and cautious in your approach to slam bidding. In (a) – in which spade contracts make 12 tricks on each of the first two deals of the rubber – it pays to be bold: the 6♠ slam bid, which makes twice, compares favourably

Slam scoring: the bold and the cautious

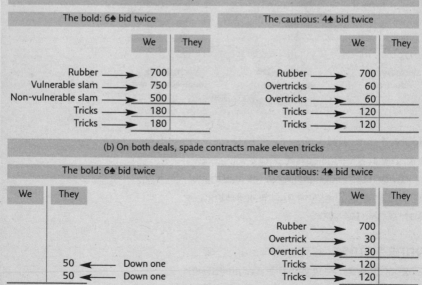

(a) On both deals, spade contracts make 12 tricks							
The bold: 6♠ bid twice				**The cautious: 4♠ bid twice**			
		We	They			We	They
Rubber	→	700		Rubber	→	700	
Vulnerable slam	→	750		Overtricks	→	60	
Non-vulnerable slam	→	500		Overtricks	→	60	
Tricks	→	180		Tricks	→	120	
Tricks	→	180		Tricks	→	120	

(b) On both deals, spade contracts make eleven tricks							
The bold: 6♠ bid twice				**The cautious: 4♠ bid twice**			
We	They					We	They
				Rubber	→	700	
				Overtrick	→	30	
				Overtrick	→	30	
	50	←	Down one	Tricks	→	120	
	50	←	Down one	Tricks	→	120	

with the more cautious 4♠ bid, also making twice. In
(b) – in which spade contracts make eleven tricks on
each of the first two deals of the rubber – it pays to
be cautious: the bold 6♠ slam bid is down one trick
on both deals compared to the cautious 4♠ bid,
which is plus one trick on both.

must know
Go for slam only if you
think you have at least
an even money chance
of succeeding.

Scoring honours

Not used in Duplicate Bridge (see p. 229), the extra
score you receive for the holding of certain honour
combinations is perhaps the quirkiest rule in the
whole game (and there's a move afoot to eliminate it
altogether). The scores are:

• If four of the five trump honours are held in
one player's hand (e.g. ace, queen, jack, ten),
then that player's partnership receives a
bonus (above the line) of 100 points.
• If all five trump honours are held in one
player's hand (i.e. ace, king, queen, jack and
ten), then that player's partnership receives a
bonus (above the line) of 150 points.
• If all four aces are held in one player's hand
in a no-trump contract (only), then that
player's partnership receives a bonus (above
the line) of 150 points.

Note that it doesn't matter whether the lucky player
is the declarer, the dummy or (less likely but entirely
possible) a defender. Nor does it matter whether the
contract succeeds or fails.

Don't forget to claim honours; claim them at any
time before the end of the rubber, but wait until the end
of a deal to avoid giving away unnecessary information.

Bridge types and systems

All modern bridge, apart from Minibridge (see p. 229), is 'Contract Bridge'. Rubber Bridge, as described in this book, is a type of Contract Bridge. Two alternative types – Chicago and Duplicate – are outlined here, along with some of the different bidding styles you may meet in other parts of the world.

must know

If you want to play a form of bridge with a fixed time limit, then choose Chicago. The tactics in Chicago are similar to Rubber Bridge, but with a big premium on bidding (and making) games.

The different varieties of the game of bridge

Chicago ('Four-Deal') Bridge

Four commuters travelling to and from Chicago loved to play bridge together on the train. The problem with Rubber Bridge is that a rubber can last anything from ten minutes (two deals – two games) to two or more hours (lots of part-scores and failing contracts). This spurred the commuters to invent a form of bridge in which precisely four deals are played – henceforth known as 'Chicago'. One Chicago tends to last just under half-an-hour, matching their 28-minute train journey perfectly.

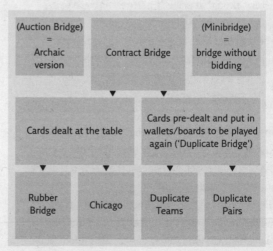

(Auction Bridge) = Archaic version	Contract Bridge	(Minibridge) = bridge without bidding
Cards dealt at the table		Cards pre-dealt and put in wallets/boards to be played again ('Duplicate Bridge')
Rubber Bridge	Chicago	Duplicate Teams	Duplicate Pairs

More and more Chicago is being played, for the reason valued by the commuters: it has a fixed duration.

Duplicate Bridge

Duplicate Bridge, another variety of Contract Bridge, uses pre-dealt cards, with each player's hand placed in a separate pocket inside a 'wallet' or in a 'board'. This enables the deal to be transported, in full, to another table, where it can be replayed.

Almost all tournament and club bridge is Duplicate Bridge. There are two types of Duplicate Bridge: Duplicate Pairs ('Pairs') or – less common – Duplicate Teams ('Teams'). In 'Pairs' you compete as a partnership, whereas in 'Teams' you compete as four players, one pair sitting North-South at a table, the other East-West at another table.

The principle of Pairs is ingenious. By the end of the session everybody has played the same hands, thus reducing the luck element of the game. Partnerships sitting 'North-South' typically stay stationary for the session; 'East-West' partnerships move to the next higher numbered table after each round.

> **must know**
> In Duplicate Bridge, competitors all play the same deals; winning is not a matter of holding better cards, but a case of doing better with the same cards.

Minibridge

Minibridge is essentially bridge without bidding. Devised in the early eighties in Holland, it's a wonderful way of introducing bridge to children, a great way to learn about the play of the cards, and indeed a very skilful game in itself.

Like bridge, minibridge is for four players seated round a table. All 52 cards are dealt. Each player counts their points and, unlike real bridge, announces their total. These should add up to 40 between the four players. One partnership will have more points (re-deal if the points are split 20-20 between the two partnerships), and within this partnership, the member with the fewest points puts her cards face up on the table and becomes the dummy. Her partner, the one with more points in the partnership, chooses a trump suit (the longest is normally best) and becomes the declarer (see the diagram below).

Minibridge

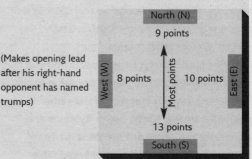

Dummy
(puts cards face up on the table, allowing partner to choose trumps)

North (N)
9 points

(Makes opening lead after his right-hand opponent has named trumps)

West (W) 8 points   Most points   10 points   East (E)

13 points
South (S)

Declarer
(has most points within the winning partnership)

must know
The English Bridge Union's website www.ebu.co.uk/education/minibridge covers all the information you need on Minibridge.

The opening lead is made by the player on the declarer's left (with dummy visible – unlike the real game), and play proceeds clockwise with the declarer (and the opponents) trying to make as many tricks as possible. There are variations of minibridge – in some, the declarer contracts to make (at least) a specific number of tricks.

Bridge systems

Bridge is bridge, whether you play it in New York, New Guinea or the New Kings Road. However there are certain differences in bidding styles (known as 'systems' or 'methods') around the world. Here are two of the most important:

• English Standard 'Acol' ('Four-card majors and weak no-trump') is prevalent in Britain, and the method I have assumed throughout this book. In the Acol system, One of a major openings can be (and frequently are) four-card suits, and a 1NT opener contains 12–14 points.

• International ('Five-card majors and strong no-trump') is almost universally played in America, France and many other countries. In this system, a One-of-a-major opener (1♥ and 1♠) guarantees five+ cards, and 1♣ and 1♦ openers can be made on three-card suits. The 1NT opener is strong (15–17 points) and Two-openers (2♦, 2♥ and 2♠) are weak (showing 5–10 points and a six-card suit). SAYC (Standard American Yellow Card) is a bidding system based on Five-card majors and a strong no-trump. It is widely used on the internet.

Being able to adjust between systems is valuable if you want to play internationally.

want to know more?

• Duplicate Bridge is a riveting game. Why not join a bridge club (see p. 233–4) and sign up for some tuition, or find a willing partner to coach you. In addition, you may like to turn to one of the recommended books on p. 234–5.
• Websites for playing bridge are listed on p. 232.
• To read more instructional pieces for the less experienced player – and much more – see www.andrewrobson.co.uk.

Further bridge resources

Websites

You can glean further information about the game, whether you are looking for books, clubs, or instructional material, on the many bridge websites. However, many websites have more to offer: you can actually play bridge!

- Here are some recommended sites where you can play bridge:

www.bridgebase.com
If I could only take one site to my desert island, this would be it. It contains a special "lounge" for beginners. For the more experienced, there is live commentary of top events worldwide, lots of useful material, and the opportunity to play online 24 hours a day. All completely free.

www.funbridge.com
Highly recommended for learning players, as well as the more experienced. One month free trial. Many of my students recommend this site.

www.bridgeclublive.com (a small annual charge for playing)
Although most internet bridge is played along international system lines (or "Standard American Yellow Card" – SAYC), this site (organised by the English Bridge Union – *see below*) sees much English-style "Acol" played.

www.okbridge.com (a small annual charge for playing)
The first bridge-playing website for a reliable, good quality game.

- Although you cannot actually play an online game, the following sites provide very good information and links to other sites:

www.ebu.co.uk
This is the website of the English Bridge Union, the organising body of duplicate bridge in England. There is much useful material here: news of tournaments, events for the less experienced player, plus the laws governing infractions (which I have deliberately omitted to dwell upon, because the game should be played for fun without seeking to benefit from such infractions).

For the rest of the United Kingdom and Ireland, see:
www.sbu.org.uk (Scotland), **www.wbu.org.uk** (Wales), **www.nibu.co.uk** (Northern Ireland), **www.cbai.ie** (Republic of Ireland).

- Here are a few other useful bridge websites – amongst many:

www.andrewrobson.co.uk   A personal favourite!
www.greatbridgelinks.com   The name says it all.
www.ecatsbridge.com   The website for "Simultaneous Pairs".
www.mrbridge.co.uk   Much useful material for sale.
www.newinbridge.com   News from around the world of top-level bridge.
www.bridgewinners.com   For the more experienced player – USA-based.

Apps

For iPhone and Android, choose from:
iBridgeBaron, iBridgeplus, Bridge Base Online, Fun Bridge, Omar Sharif Bridge. Although £13.99 to buy, I recommend Bridge Baron.

Software

There are CDs that enable you to play an endless supply of randomly generated deals. Amongst the best on the market, all of which can be programmed to play English Standard Acol, are:

Blue Chip (especially recommended)
Q-Plus
Bridge Baron
GIB
Jack

And then there are CDs that do not have a playing engine, but feature structured learning based on set deals. My favourite of these are...

- For declarer-play practice:

Bridgemaster 2000 with Fred Gitelman (the brain behind Bridgebase)
Counting at Bridge with Mike Lawrence

- For bidding:

Acol Bidding with Bernard Magee

- For defence:

Modern Bridge Defence with Eddie Kantar

- Personal favourites:

What Should Have Happened with Andrew Robson
The *Bridge Lessons* series with Andrew Robson

Playing on your home computer is very rewarding, but I'm sure you will soon want to venture into...

Bridge clubs

You can get the full club listings through the websites listed above. Most bridge clubs focus entirely on duplicate bridge, but all sensible ones know that their future is dependent on encouraging the less experienced, through classes, practice sessions, and duplicates aimed specifically at learners.

Here is an extensive (but not exhaustive) listing of beginner-friendly clubs:

- England:

Club name	Tel no	Website/email address
Acol Bridge Club	020 7624 7407	www.acolbridgeclub.com
Andrew Robson Bridge Club	020 7471 4626	www.andrewrobson.co.uk
Aylesbury Vale Bridge Club	07710 867982	www.aylesburyvalebridge.com
Blewbury Bridge Club	01235 851403	via www.blewbury.co.uk
Brevion Bridge Club, Chelmsford	01245 222393	www.brevion-bridge.co.uk
Bristol Bridge Club	0117 929 1846	www.bristolbridgeclub.co.uk
Manchester Bridge Club	0161 4453712	www.manchesterbridge.co.uk
Richmond Bridge Club (Surrey)	01276 471084	juneaknott@onetel.com
Peterborough Bridge Club	01733 572457	www.peterboroughbridge.info
St George's Bridge Centre, Darlington	01325 360340	www.stgeorgesbridge.co.uk
South Bucks Bridge Centre	01628 668700	www.southbucksbridgecentre.co.uk

West Midlands Bridge Club, Solihull	0121 704 9633	www.westmidbridge.co.uk
Welwyn Garden City BC	01438 840821	www.wgcbridge.org.uk
Wilton Bridge Club, Taunton	01823 400418	via www.somersetbridge.org.uk
Winchester Novice Bridge Club	01420 561548	www.dianaharveybridge.net
Worcester Bridge Club	01905 25265	www.bridgewebs.com/worcester
Young Chelsea Bridge Club	020 7373 1665	www.ycbc.co.uk

- *Scotland:*

Club name	Tel no	Website/address
The Bridge Club, Aberdeen	01224 644773	14 Rubislaw Terrace, Aberdeen AB10 1XE
Dundee Bridge Club	01628 668700	www.dundeebridgeclub.co.uk
Buchanan Bridge Club, Glasgow	0141 3325131	4 Clairmont Gardens, Glasgow, G3 7LW

- *Wales:*

Club name	Tel no	Website
Cardiff Bridge Club	029 20491865	www.penylanclub.org.uk
Swansea Bridge Club	01792 466 965	www.swanseabridgeclub.org.uk

- *Ireland:*

Club name	Tel no	Website/address
The Regent, Dublin	+ 353 (0)1 6684194	www.bridgewebs.com/regent
The Hamilton Bridge Club, Limerick	061 325880	Monument Bridge Club, Hamilton House, Roxboro Road, Limerick
Bantry Bridge Club, Cork	027 51495	JJ Crowleys Bar, Wolfe Tone Square, Bantry

Specialist outlets

So much is done over the internet these days, but you can visit London's Chess and Bridge where you can browse to your heart's content:

Chess and Bridge
44 Baker Street
London
W1U 7RT
Tel: 020 7486 8222
www.chess.co.uk

Books

So many bridge books have been written, the most popular of all being Ely Culberston's wonderful *Red Book on Play*, published way back in 1934 (my first inspiration – now out of print).

Here is my selection of some of the best (with some bias!):

For the less experienced:

The Really Easy series   The English Bridge Union
Begin Bridge with Reese   Terence Reese
Improve Your Bridge Game   Andrew Robson
What Should Have Happened   Andrew Robson

● For the more advanced:

Play These Hands With Me   Terence Reese
Why You Lose at Bridge   Skid Simon
How to Read Your Opponents' Cards   Mike Lawrence
The Bridge Lessons series (18 booklets)   Andrew Robson

● For entertainment:

Bridge My Way   Zia Mahmood
Tales from the Bridge Table   John Clay
Bridge in the Menagerie   Victor Mollo

● Other classics:

Bridge is an Easy Game   Ian Macleod
The Great Bridge Scandal   Alan Truscott
Story of an Accusation   Terence Reese

The last two expound the case for and against Boris Schapiro and Terence Reese (himself) cheating in the 1965 World Championships. Read Truscott and you're convinced they did it; read Reese and you're positive they didn't!

Terence Reese is without doubt one of the most compelling bridge writers – and I didn't even mention his gripping *The Expert Game*. I would like to mention three other writers too: David Bird, Ron Klinger, and Andrew Kambites.

Although bridge books for experienced players are plentiful, there's a dearth of books at the beginner end of the market, which I hope this book has gone some way to remedying.

Magazines
Membership of a Home Bridge Union will include a regular magazine. Here are other specialist magazines:

Bridge Magazine: Online only. **www.bridgemagazine.co.uk** or ring 020 7388 2404.

Bridge: A free publication with some good articles – although mainly a selling tool for Mr Bridge. See **www.mrbridge.co.uk** or ring 01483 489961 to order a copy.

above A score that goes above the line, not counting towards game.

Acol The bidding system used in Great Britain, based loosely around a weak no-trump and four-card majors.

Auction Bridge Archaic version, where credit towards game is given for all tricks, whether contracted for or not.

auction Bidding.

balanced Shape of hand with no void, no singleton and not more than one doubleton.

below A score that goes below the line, i.e. bid and made.

bidding First phase of the game in which players try to describe their hands using a special code.

Blackwood The most famous convention. A bid of Four no-trumps (4NT) asks partner for their number of aces.

board Used in Duplicate Bridge with separate slots for the four hands, for movement of cards to another table.

Chicago Four-deal bridge, with cards dealt at the table.

competitive auction Both sides bid.

Contract Bridge All modern forms. Involves gaining points towards game only for those tricks bid and made.

convention Special bid, by partnership agreement, whose meaning is not connected to the mentioned suit (or no-trumps).

cue-bidding Bidding suits not based on length, but (typically) whether they have the ace (or king).

cut Splitting of the pack prior to dealing.

declarer By being the first to bid the trump suit (or no-trumps) in the first phase of the game, this player goes on to control both his cards and dummy's (opposite) in the play.

discard Playing a card that doesn't involve following to the suit led, nor trumping.

distribution The four different suit lengths within a hand; or the same suit divided around the table.

double A call (bid) that raises the stakes of success or failure of the doubled contract (although in many contexts it means something entirely different – asking partner to bid).

doubleton Two cards in a suit.

draw trumps Play trumps to remove the opposing trumps.

duck Play low, when playing higher was possible.

dummy Partner of the declarer, this player tables his cards after the opening lead, and takes no further role until the next deal.

Duplicate Bridge Form of bridge in which the same deal is played at more than one table. 'Pairs' and 'Teams' are two types of Duplicate Bridge.

dustbin 1NT The One no-trump (1NT) response – a weak bid with hands that don't fit anywhere else.

East-West One partnership, typically the two defenders.

EBU English Bridge Union – governing body of Duplicate Bridge in England.

English Standard Modern English bidding methods, based on Acol.

finesse Card promotion technique, depending for its success on the relative position of the card you are trying to promote, and the opposing higher card.

fit A mutually agreeable trump suit (requires eight+ cards).

Five-card majors A bidding system in which the 1♥/1♠ opener guarantees five+ cards.

force Method of making extra tricks by flushing out an opposing higher card to promote lower cards.

forcing A bid that forces partner to bid again.

fourth highest (. . . of your longest and strongest suit). Normal opening lead versus no-trumps.

game Requires 100 points to make game. Two games are required to make a rubber, the ultimate goal in Rubber Bridge.

game contract One of the following: 3NT, 4♥, 4♠, 5♣, 5♦.

grand slam The jackpot in bridge. Involves bidding Seven-of-something and scoring a big bonus if successful.

hand The cards held by an individual player.

honour The top five cards of each suit: ace, king, queen, jack and the ten.

honours Used in Rubber Bridge and Chicago, giving bonuses for one hand holding four/five of the trump honours, or all four aces in no-trumps.

intermediates Tens and nines (and eights).

invitational bid Bid that invites partner to the next zone – game (or slam).

jump Bid unnecessarily high, missing (at least) one lower level.

jump raise Bid that agrees with partner's suit, missing out (at least) one level.

length Method of making extra tricks by exhausting the opponents of all of their cards in a suit.

level of the fit When the number of trumps held by the partnership equals the number of tricks for which the partnership has bid in that suit.

limit bid Bid that limits the strength of the hand.

major The higher-ranking and higher-scoring two suits: spades and hearts.

Minibridge Form of bridge without bidding.

minor The lower-ranking and lower-scoring two suits: diamonds and clubs.

misfit When there is no suit in which there is a fit (for either side).

negative Weak response to (say) a Two-of-a-suit opener.

no bid *See* pass.

North-South One partnership, typically declarer (South) and dummy (North).

no-trumps Playing without a trump suit; ranked higher than the four suits.

one-suiter Hand with one long (i.e. six+ card) suit.

opener The player who opens the bidding (pass not counting).

opening lead First card played – by the player on the declarer's left. The only card played before dummy is tabled.

overcall Bid after the opponents have opened the bidding.

overtricks Extra tricks made above the number contracted.

Pairs Duplicate Bridge where you compete as a partnership.

part-score Contract that does not give game.

part-score carryover The part-score carries over to the next deal. Always in Rubber; never in Duplicate; optional in Chicago.

pass As 'no bid', the call that opts out of making a (higher) bid.

passed hand Hand that could not open the bidding.

penalty Points conceded (perhaps doubled) by failing to make a contract.

penalty double Call expressing confidence that the opposing contract will fail, increasing the score (of failure and success).

Phoney Stayman Using Stayman with intention of bailing into 3♣ as a weakness take-out into clubs.

point count Ace = four; king = three; queen = two; jack (knave) = one.

pre-empt Space-consuming bid made to disrupt opponents, typically made with a weak hand.

quacks Queens and jacks.

quick tricks Aces, and ace-kings.

rank Suit order. Working upwards: clubs, diamonds, hearts, spades, no-trumps.

rebid Second bid of a player.

redouble Only legal after an opponent has doubled, this doubles the score of a doubled contract (success or failure).

responder Opener's partner during the bidding.

reverse Bid of second suit (typically by opener) that pushes responder to the Three level in order to give preference back to the first suit.

revoke Not follow suit when it is possible to do so.

rubber Two games.

ruffing Trumping.

ruffing value Trump potential via a short side-suit (doubleton or less).

Rule of 14 Guideline for responding in a new suit at the Two level, requiring your length in the suit added to your total point count to reach 14.

Rule of 20 Guideline for opening the bidding – when high-card points added to lengths of two longest suits reaches 20.

Rule of One Guideline to leave the master trump outstanding.

Glossary

sacrificing Bidding a contract in which you expect to fail, in order to prevent the opponents from declaring a contract you expect them to make.

SAYC Standard American Yellow Card – bidding system widely used on the internet, based on Five-card majors and a strong no-trump.

sequence Two or more touching cards, where the higher is an honour (ten or above).

shape The lengths of the four suits within a bridge hand.

shortage Lacking cards in a particular suit.

side suit A non-trump suit.

signal A defensive card that sends a message to partner.

Simultaneous Pairs Duplicate Pairs events, where the same boards are used country/worldwide.

single major raise One of the following bids: 1♠-2♠ or 1♥-2♥.

singleton One card in a suit.

slam Six or Seven-level contract – normally six (i.e. small).

small slam Bidding Six-of-something, scoring a vulnerability-related bonus if successful.

SOS Three requirements for a take-out double (support, opening points and shortage).

split Division of missing cards of a suit.

spot card Card identified by the number of suit symbols depicted. Each suit contains ten spot cards.

SQOT Suit Quality Overcall Test – a measure of whether a suit is good enough to overcall.

Stayman Conventional 2♣ response to a One no-trump (1NT) opener (or 3♣ to 2NT), requesting a four-card major.

stopper Way of stopping the opponents running though a suit (typically in no-trumps).

strong no-trump A 15–17 point One no-trump (1NT) opener (occasionally 16–18 point).

strong Two A Two-level opener showing around 20–22 points and a good five (six) card suit.

system A whole bidding method, such as Acol.

take-out Removing to a different bid.

take-out double Call asking partner to bid.

teams Duplicate Bridge where you compete as a team-of-four.

the line Horizontal line, midway down Rubber score-pad. Only points towards game go below the line.

three-suiter Hand with the (dreaded) 4441 shape.

top tricks Those tricks that can be made before losing the lead.

trick One card from each player, each following to the suit led where possible.

trump Boss suit, one per deal (unless no-trumps), determined by being the last suit bid.

Two clubs Conventional opener showing any hand with 23+ points.

two-suiter Hand with two long suits (i.e. five-four or longer).

unbalanced Shape of hand with either a void, a singleton, or more than one doubleton.

undertricks Number of tricks by which the contract failed.

Universal Bidding Rules Recommended guidelines for all players: (i) Repeating a suit shows six cards. (ii) Bidding two suits shows five-four or better.

void Holding no cards in a suit.

vulnerable Having one game towards rubber, increasing the bonus for game (playing Chicago/Duplicate), slam (all forms), and the loss for undertricks.

weakness take-out Removing partner's One no-trump (1NT) opener to Two-of-a-suit.

weak no-trump A 12–14 point One no-trump opener.

weak Two A Two-level opener, by agreement, showing a six-card suit and around 5–10 points.

whist Trick-taking game without a dummy.

Yarborough Hand with no high-card points or tens.

zone Part-score, game or slam.